hicago to Los Angeles
ril 1, 1943

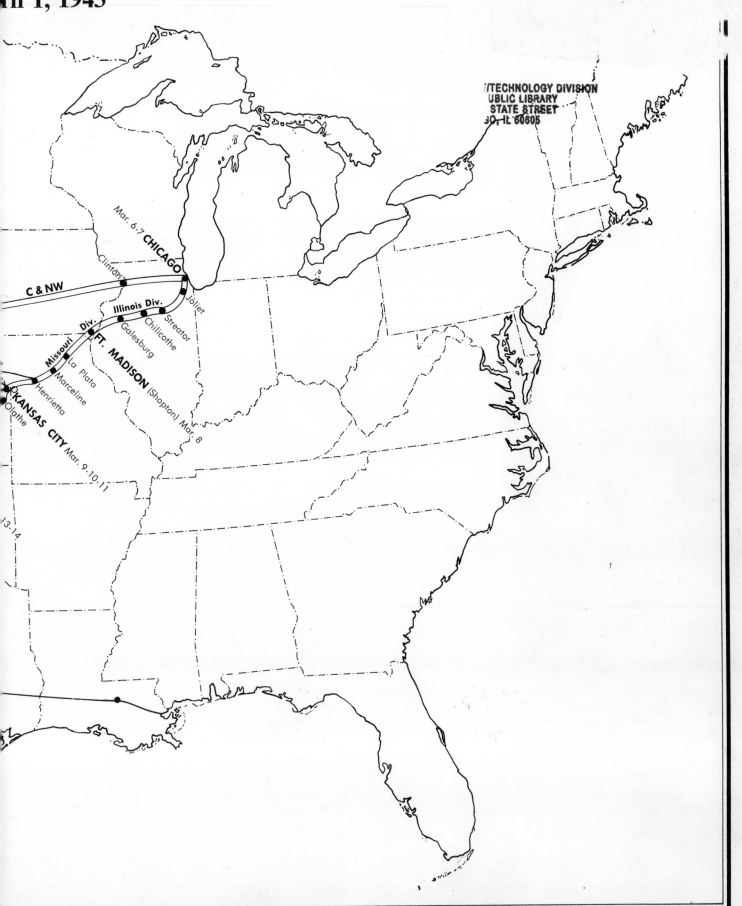

Mar. 6-7 **CHICAGO**

Clinton

C & NW

Illinois Div.

Joliet

Streator

Chillcothe

Galesburg

Div.

Missouri

La Plata

FT. MADISON (Shopton) Mar. 8

Marceline

Henrietta

KANSAS CITY Mar. 9-10-11

Olathe

13-14

The

IRON HORSE

at WAR

Just prior to departing the Burlington's yards at Cicero, Illinois, a veteran hogger thrusts his long spouted oiler into the openings of a Boxpok drivered Q-5a Northern to lubricate shoes and wedges.

The
IRON HORSE at WAR

The United States Government's Photodocumentary
Project on American Railroading During the
Second World War

by JAMES E. VALLE

WITH 272 OF ITS PHOTOGRAPHS BY JACK DELANO

BERKELEY Howell-North Books CALIFORNIA

THE IRON HORSE AT WAR

Printed and bound in the United States of America

Library of Congress Catalog Card No. 77-075624

ISBN No. 0-8310-7112-5

Second Edition, June 1978

For Eddie and Suzanne

Published by Howell-North Books
1050 Parker Street, Berkeley, California 94710

Introduction

The four years of American participation in the Second World War wrote a unique and dramatic chapter in the history of railroading. After long years of Depression-bred neglect and stagnation, the railroad industry was suddenly confronted with a task of heroic proportions. A vast flood of traffic, raw materials, fuels, munitions, weapons, and an enormous quantity of foodstuffs and manufactured items of every size and description had to be moved quickly and efficiently so that a global war effort could be nourished and sustained. In addition to the crushing volume of freight there was also an enormous increase in passenger traffic. Troop trains crammed with fresh-faced inductees shared the main lines with commuter runs, accommodations, and name trains running in multiple sections as a public suddenly flush with defense plant prosperity sought to preserve cherished American mobility in the face of gasoline and tire rationing.

This tremendous surge of traffic coincided with the final years of the long kingship of steam traction in the United States. Although a few road Diesels were slowly being introduced into main-line service and the ubiquitous internal combustion switch engine was increasingly in evidence, whole divisions and even entire railroads were still purely steam operations. Old but reliable Consolidations and Mikados shared honors with some of the most modern and impressive examples of the locomotive builder's art, for this was the prime of life for the fleets of Hudson, Texas, and Northern types that would one day close out the steam era. Huge-boilered and long-gutted behemoths incorporating every refinement known to internal expansion, these locomotives performed prodigies of useful labor and, together with their lesser brethren,

created a vast panorama of smoke-erupting, ear-splitting action.

It was a Golden Age for the *afficionados* of the Iron Horse and many of them haunted the tracksides and depots, camera in hand, to record the scene for posterity. Of this legion of shutterbugs, perhaps none was granted the opportunity to make such a complete and definitive study as Jack Delano, a young lensman working on assignment for the United States Office of War Information (OWI). Utilizing his official credentials to their fullest extent, Delano haunted roundhouses, freight yards, passenger depots, dispatchers' offices, repair shops, engine cabs, cabooses, and interlocking towers with complete freedom to record everything visible, and at government expense! It was the opportunity of a lifetime and it was not wasted for Delano brought to his task the skills and traditions of the great age of governmental documentary photography and combined them with his own keen interest in all phases of workaday life. The result was a fine collection of prints that captures the full scope and drama of the apogee of American railroading.

The core of Delano's work falls into two distinct phases. He began his assignment in and around Chicago in November 1942, recording the vast variety and enormous amount of railroad activity of this largest and busiest of the nation's transportation hubs with particular emphasis on the Chicago and North Western Railway and the Indiana Harbor Belt Line. When he had covered the Chicago scene to his satisfaction, he next embarked on a 2000-mile journey across the Midwest, Southwest, and Far West as a guest of the Santa Fe Railroad. During this trip, Delano made every effort to record the essence of railroading

5

as it was experienced by the men who operated the trains, depots, towers, and servicing facilities. When he concluded his trip in Los Angeles he had among his rolls of exposed film, sequences of railroad action such as an ordinary fan might not capture in a lifetime of dedicated effort. Above all, he had recorded the human element of railroading in the candid, naturalistic style that was the hallmark of the OWI project and its great predecessor, the Farm Services Administration documentaries of the 1930s.

Since so much of the action captured by Delano's camera takes place on the Santa Fe, a few remarks concerning this legendary system are in order. Originally organized in 1868, the Atchison, Topeka & Santa Fe Railroad had grown from a few score miles of unballasted light iron spiked down on dry Kansas prairie to a transcontinental giant. By 1943 it was a railroad of considerable diversity and character, possessed of a vast stable of motive power and a wide variety of operating conditions, deserts, mountains, flatlands, and big city terminals. Its locomotive roster was populated by some of the oldest as well as some of the newest engines to be found in mainline service, sprightly Atlantics and Prairies that had helped pull Death Valley Scotty's *Coyote Special* back in 1905 working in tandem with enormous 3750 class Northerns and F T units doled out to the road by a tight-fisted War Production Board. Unlike most Western roads, the Santa Fe had no indigenous Mallets on its roster although a few Norfolk and Western Giants were borrowed at the height of the wartime emergency together with some Boston and Maine Berkshires looking very out of place under the hot Southwestern sun. Diesel switchers were much in evidence on the Santa Fe's property and Mikados dominated the freight power pools east of New Mexico.

To the motive power esthete Santa Fe steam was made distinctive by the road's preference for very large-diameter boilers which, especially with the newer engines, stretched bridge and tunnel clearances to the limits and even required the fitting of retractable smokestacks. Also noteworthy were the large square tenders and double sandboxes which, together with engine number boards mounted just behind the stack, were a common feature of the road's power and created a massive, bulky effect that did little justice to the great resources of speed and endurance possessed by the newest Santa Fe steamers. Seventy-four-inch drivers enabled Texas-type freight hogs to maintain express schedules while the Northerns were renowned for their ability to wheel solid strings of all-steel coaches across 1700 miles of mountain and desert, changing crews eight times between engine terminals.

The Santa Fe's contribution to the war effort was fully in keeping with its massive locomotives and far-flung trackage. Revenue train miles, which had stood at 40.9 million in 1938 spiraled to 70.7 million by 1945. Since this vast traffic had to be moved in the face of one of the worst manpower shortages in American history, hundreds of youths and women were hired to do light work around the shops and roundhouses and to fill in as brakemen and firemen on the much expanded extra boards. Heavy track repairs were handled by gangs of Mexican nationals and Indians drawn from the many reservations located in the Santa Fe's bailiwick. That these improbable railroaders, together with the older, experienced "rails" who formed the hard core of the company's manpower, contrived to deliver the goods, represents a dramatic tour de force in the annals of American Railroading.

Acknowledgments

■■

Because this volume is an attempt to recreate the image of American railroading during a specific historical epoch, it was made possible only by the diligence and forethought of two specific groups of people, those who originated the basic idea of a photodocumentary project on the subject of railroading in 1942 and those who preserved the resulting collection of prints and made them available to the Author some thirty-two years later.

Of the first group, honors are due to Roy Stryker who, during his long and distinguished tenure as supervisor of Governmental Documentary Photography, has presided over the creation of pictorial essays of unsurpassed technical quality and artistic genius. In compiling the collection presented here, Stryker's organization, the Photographic Section of the Office of War Information, received much valuable assistance from the Association of American Railroads which arranged for the securing of passes and clearances and acted as liason between the Government's personnel and the individual railroad companies. Three railroads in particular, the Chicago and North Western, the Indiana Harbor Belt, and the Atchison, Topeka and Santa Fe, were particularly generous with their facilities and cooperation. The Santa Fe was perhaps the most cordial of all, providing Public Relations Department escorts and instructing division superintendents, trainmasters, and operating personnel all along its far-flung right of way to extend every possible courtesy to the photographer.

Much later, in the winter of 1974 to be exact, the collection was discovered by Richard Rothman, an ex-college-roommate and lifelong friend of mine, while he was searching through the holdings of the Prints and Photographs Division of the Library of Congress for materials relating to the Farm Services Administration. The job of sifting this unexpected bonanza and reproducing the materials for subsequent publication brought me into contact with the second group, the curators of the combined FAS - OWI Collection. Particular kindness was shown me by Jerry Kearns and by Leroy Bellamy whose cheerful willingness to explain the intricacies of the Library of Congress' photoduplication procedures greatly facilitated the production of this manuscript.

Between these two groups, one man served as the essential link with the past. The photographer, Jack Delano, now living in Puerto Rico where he is active in a wide range of artistic and creative endeavors, enthusiastically volunteered to supply valuable materials and reminiscences which proved enormously helpful in recreating the historical details of the events herein recorded. His wholehearted cooperation was not only a technical advantage to me but provided an important element of encouragement to sustain the project.

Finally, several other persons provided assistance in various capacities. Bill Burk of the Santa Fe's Office of Public Relations supplied much vital statistical information and some interesting graphic materials. Helen Duff, a good friend and professional colleague shared memories of her experiences as a wartime railroad passenger while Kathleen Beerhalter and Glenn Sturge provided technical advice concerning the processing and publication of photographs.

Without the assistance of all these men and women, the creation of this book would have been immensely more difficult and the results far less satisfactory.

JAMES E. VALLE

February 8, 1976
Dover, Delaware

7

Contents

Introduction 5

Acknowledgments 7

Prologue 9

Chicago Union Station, 1943 35

Proviso Yard 45

"One Hundred Miles . . . Shall Constitute a Day's Work" . 79

An Indiana Harbor Belt Album 97

Midwestern Miscellany 114

A Journey Begins: Chicago to Kansas City 123

Central Kansas and Oklahoma 143

The Belen Cutoff 169

Diesels Across the Desert 195

California 215

Jack Delano's Written Accounts 250

Index 256

Prologue

■■

The photographs on the following pages are the work of several men and women who contributed to the Farm Services Administration and Office of War Information projects on American Life in the early 1940s. Although none of these government photographers was, strictly speaking, a railfan, all of them were concerned with capturing the essence and spirit of America and each grasped that the railroad scene was a central facet of the American character. For this reason, the systematic coverage initiated by Jack Delano was preceded by many earlier individual efforts on the part of such skilled artists as Marion Post Wolcott, Russell Lee, John Vachon, and the late Dorothea Lange, among others.

A gallery of their work is presented here in order to establish the antecedents of the Delano Collection and so that the reader may enjoy the brilliant quality and artistic excellence of a collection not previously available to the average railfan.

9

This diminutive "Bull of the Woods" was captured by the camera of Russell Lee in deepest Michigan in 1937. Note the snow flanges mounted on the pilot and the well-polished voluminous spark arrester on the stack. (*FSA Photo*)

Perhaps the last sort of engine that any sensible railroader would select for switching and transfer service among the cane fields and sugar refineries of South Central Florida would be a high-drivered light Pacific. Yet, here comes No. 98 rolling down the rickety iron of the United States Sugar Company's operation at Clewiston with several car-loadings of cane and pulp tied to her tank. For those who enjoy tracing the origins of secondhand motive power, No. 98 is no challenge at all. The identifying marks of the Florida East Coast Line are stamped all over her. (*FSA Photo: Marion Post Wolcott*)

In 1940, headquarters for the Virginia & Truckee Railroad were located at Carson City, Nevada, where, in its heyday as the principal route to the fabulous Comstock silver lode, a large complex of shops and roundhouses stabled motive power of great character and diversity. When this scene was recorded by FSA photographer Arthur Rothstein the rich veins running under Virginia City were long since played out and the V & T had shrunk to the merest shadow of its former self. It seemed determined, however, to perpetuate a host of anachronisms, banjo switches, square steam chests, wooden clerestory-roofed baggage cars and coaches, and the rare three-way stub turnout in the foreground. Although time is rapidly running out, pride and morale is still high enough among the employees to see to it that the brass band under the stack cap of Ten Wheeler No. 26 is well polished for the daily run to Reno with the afternoon mixed.

This group of views was taken by Russell Lee along the route of the Rio Grande Southern during September, 1940. By that time, the RGS was already defunct as a corporate entity but traffic still rolled along some of its narrow-gauge rails under the auspices of the Denver and Rio Grande Western which supplied motive power in the form of its Durango based "Mudhen" 2-8-2s. Typical of this diminutive tribe is No. 453 which has just arrived in Telluride with an assortment of antiquated rolling stock and RGS caboose No. 402.

The reason for this continuation of service long past the point of natural expiration was that several mines along the RGS were producing rare and highly-prized ores that figured heavily in certain experiments that were being conducted in deepest secrecy in connection with nuclear fission and the harnessing of the atom. With war unmistakably looming on the horizon, this was a high-priority operation and because of it, the Rio Grande Southern was reprieved.

13

Durango (left) has always billed itself as the "Narrow Gauge Capital of the World" and this claim is largely justified for in its prime as a municipality the slim gauge iron radiated outwards from it like the cardinal points of a compass. As the narrow gauge empire shrank, Durango became the nucleus of what remained and thus a repository for increasingly rare motive power. Here, three Denver and Rio Grande Western locomotives, each representing a different generation of slim-gauge power, sit placidly in the engine house awaiting the Engine Dispatcher's call. No. 268, a 2-8-0 dating back to the 1880s will probably draw nothing more demanding than a stint as yard goat around the terminal. Consolidation No. 375 could still look forward to road service as a passenger engine, perhaps on the San Juan running daily between Durango and Alamosa. Mudhen No. 459 represented heavy freight power in this part of Colorado and was liable to be sent anywhere.

The depot at Ouray is tucked away on a branch line of the Denver and Rio Grande Western that originated at Montrose and reached the town via Ridgway which was the northern terminus of the Rio Grande Southern. By 1941 traffic on the Ouray Branch was infrequent and the house tracks are rapidly going to rust and weed. On the other hand, the brilliantly improvised motor locomotive No. 2, shown here in storage at Durango, can look forward to at least the prospect of a major overhaul and a few years of continued use. Passenger and mail traffic too thin to be economically serviced by conventional trains but nevertheless indispensable to the isolated towns along the RGS mainline brought No. 2 and several sisters into existence. Affectionate patrons soon christened them the "Galloping Geese" in honor of the reckless speed with which they negotiated the curves, trestles and snow sheds of Lizard Head and the peculiar swaying surging motion that the rough narrow gauge track imparted to their automotive style suspensions.

15

This heavy eight-wheeled switching and transfer locomotive posed for the camera of Arthur Rothstein at St. Louis, Mo., in 1939. *(FSA Photo)*

At Montrose, Colorado, 80 miles north of Durango, the exclusive domain of the Narrow Gauge ends and three-rail operation signals the advancing encroachments of full-scale railroading. Engine No. 781 is shown here arriving with the *Mountaineer,* an overnight train running between Montrose and Denver via Grand Junction with Pullman sleeper, day coach, and, as the presence of the express messenger on the platform indicates, mail. No. 781 is a Class T-29 Ten Wheeler built by Brooks in 1909. By 1940, when these photos were taken, some of her numerous sisters had already gone to the torch and she herself was perhaps a year short of retirement. *(FSA Photos: Russell Lee)*

Logging railroads possess a mystique all their own, particularly for those who revel in the genius of rough-and-ready improvisation. After all, what could possibly be more diverting than a woodburning narrow-gauge Heisler with a donkey winch on the pilot deck and a front coupler designed to accommodate either knuckles or links on two levels. Add to this a Dolly Varden stack and a complete absence of numbers or corporate lettering and you capture the very essence of backwoods seat-of-the-pants railroading. Russell Lee photographed this collection of anomalies somewhere in Baker County, Oregon in May 1941. *(FSA Photo)*

On a fine day in indian summer the Bangor and Aroostook's accommodation *(top right)* is pulling into the house track at Caribou, Maine. This photo was made by Jack Delano while he was working on assignment for the FSA in 1940.

As an integral slice of small-town Americana, nothing in railroading ever quite matched the charm and satisfaction of the branch line local. A downgraded road engine, some obsolete heavyweight baggage cars and coaches, and a phlegmatic easy-going crew that usually knew the passengers by name, and frequently outnumbered them, made for railroading on a human scale. Here, a typical representative of the species rambles along the Baltimore and Ohio's Portsmouth Branch in Southern Ohio. The motive power is a Class B-8 Ten Wheeler outshopped in 1893. *(OWI Photo: Arthur Siegel)*

Dorothea Lange made this photo of a Union Pacific brakeman setting out with a red flag and a cannister of torpedos and fusees to protect the rear of his train, laid out for some unknown reason while traversing the High Plains of Wyoming. *(FSA Photo)*

(left, top) Although the Santa Fe claims to have built the first ten-coupled engine with a four-wheeled trailing truck, the Texas and Pacific pioneered the large scale introduction of the 2-10-4 into modern steam railroading and locomotives of this wheel arrangement were known as "Texas" types for as long as steam lasted in the United States. FSA photographer Russell Lee made this fine study of T. & P. No. 640 at Big Spring, Texas in March, 1940, taking particular care to delineate the massively counterweighted drivers and rods that were, along with a plethora of large diameter piping, a hallmark of Texas & Pacific practice in the days of steam. One hopes that the wipers will have time to do something about the disgraceful condition of the main rod and valve gear before this hog is sent out on the road again. Nothing detracts from a steam locomotive's appearance quite as much as streaked, oil-smeared running gear!

Nestled deep in the heart of the Yew Mountains of West Virginia, Richwood is the terminus of a line that originates on the Banks of the Kanawha River, branching off from the main stem of the Baltimore and Ohio's route to Charleston via the Elk and Tygart River valleys. Here, Light Pacific No. 5123 is sitting quietly at the Richwood station waiting to start her daily trip north. Coal tipple feeder lines radiate from this branch in great profusion assuring that our humble accommodation will meet and pass many drags of loads and empties, enjoying unquestioned superiority over them all, before she terminates her run and delivers her passengers to their connections. No. 5123 was built by Baldwin in 1913 and retired in 1952. Passenger service on the Richwood Branch did not survive her by any length of time. (FSA Photo: John Collier)

A crew with its mind on "goin' to beans" has spotted this heavy Texas and Pacific switcher on the engine service track at Big Spring. By sheer accident the pose is a rods-down classic. (FSA Photo: Russell Lee)

One of the few useful developments to come out of the Federal Government's experiment in running the nation's railroads during World War I was a series of well designed and proportioned locomotives built to plans and specifications developed by the United States Railway Administration. The Nashville, Chattanooga, and St. Louis' No. 561, seen here as she picks up speed after stopping for a crew change and routine servicing at Chattanooga, was one of a group of engines whose design was based on the USRA light Mountain type. Developed by Baldwin for the N. C. & St. L., their special province was the 288-mile run between Nashville and Atlanta over the demanding Cumberland Mountain grades. (OWI Photo: Al Palmer)

23

A Los Angeles to San Diego passenger train, possibly the *San Diegan*, is pulling into her southern terminus on a bright winter day in 1943. Her locomotive, Mountain type No. 3749 is typical of the Santa Fe's second-string passenger power. She is one of a series built by Baldwin in 1924 and held such crack assignments as the *Chief* throughout the 1920s and early 1930s before being bumped to more humble runs by the arrival of the first fleet of Northerns. In compliance with stringent Southern California smoke abatement requirements, her stack is absolutely clear. *(FSA Photo: Russell Lee)*

Chattanooga is one of the American Southeast's major centers of mountain railroading, a town situated in the Tennessee River Valley between the crests of the Appalachians at just the right location to serve as a gateway to Memphis, Birmingham, New Orleans, Mobile, and the industrial centers of the Ohio Valley. As such, it was the location of one of the Southern Railway's most important pools of road and helper power. Such is the occupation of these two uncharacteristically grimy Mikes caught in the act of drifting down to the ready tracks to pick up a train. No. 6317 was built at Alco's Richmond Works and spent most of her life running between Chattanooga and Memphis on the Cincinnati, New Orleans & Texas Pacific. *(OWI Photo: Al Palmer)*

OWI lensman Jack Hollem made this fine study of the Baltimore and Ohio's brand new T-3 class Mountain type No. 5555 as she galloped through Halethorp, Md., in 1942. Unlike most U.S. railroads, the B & O never showed much interest in the 4-8-4 and chose instead to continue development of their T series 4-8-2s when the need for modern dual purpose motive power was felt. The 5555 was built in the Company's own Mt. Clare shops and had a sister, No. 5510, which was equipped with a water tube boiler, an experiment that failed miserably.

This view of the Chattanooga yards, taken in August, 1942, needs little further elaboration. Probably the railroads of the United States will never again experience the congestion and shortages that they faced in the months after Pearl Harbor. (*OWI Photo: Al Palmer*)

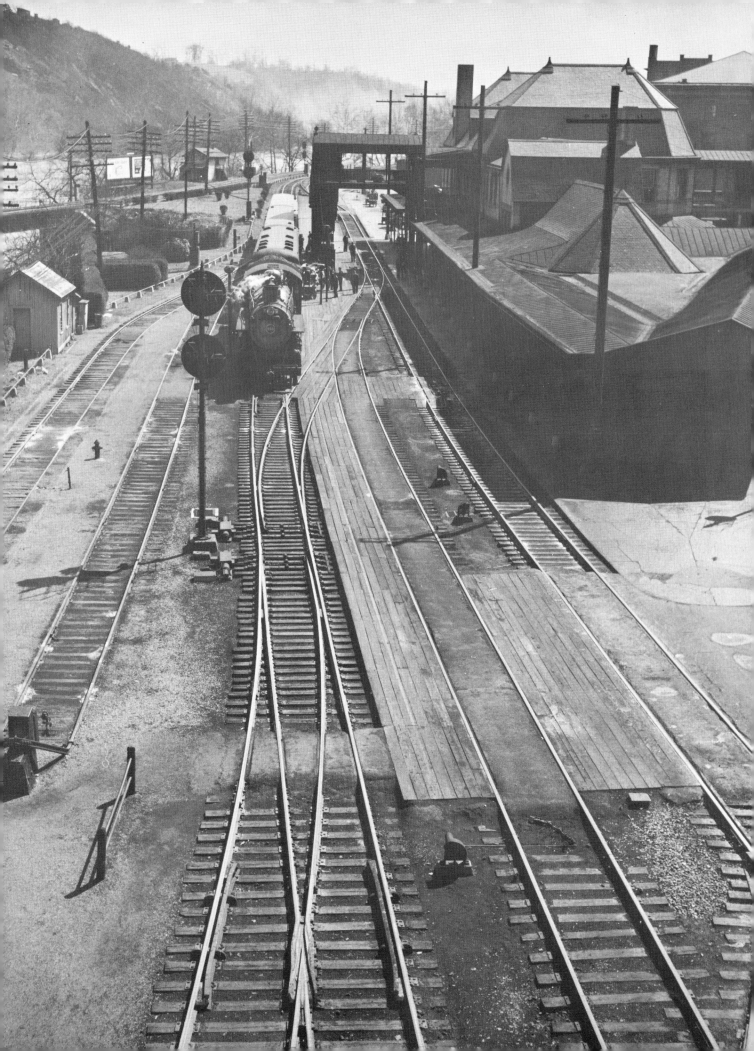

It's train time in Lynchburg, Virginia, and there is activity on the station platform, particularly in the vicinity of the baggage car. This humble accommodation is running on the Norfolk and Western's heavily traveled main stem connecting the coal tipples and feeder lines of Appalachia with the vast loading docks at Norfolk. House tracks and sidings are uncharacteristically clear on this March day in 1943.

The St. Louis and San Francisco Railroad was a line that commanded the deepest respect and admiration of all who loved well proportioned and carefully groomed motive power in the days of steam. In this picture, a trio of 4100 class Mikados, originally low drivered 2-10-2s extensively rebuilt in the road's Springfield shops, are spotted on service tracks at the Tulsa Roundhouse. No. 4103 has her rods taken down and probably won't be going anywhere today but the 4149 is almost ready for the road. We say almost because her bell is still being polished. On the Frisco, bells were a special mark of distinction, chromed on the outside and painted red inside. They symbolized the pride that the Company took in operating some of the handsomest locomotives in the nation. The slender little gadgets attached to the front of the smokestacks are lights which, turned on at night, allow the firemen to judge the thickness of their engine smoke. (*OWI Photos: John Vachon*)

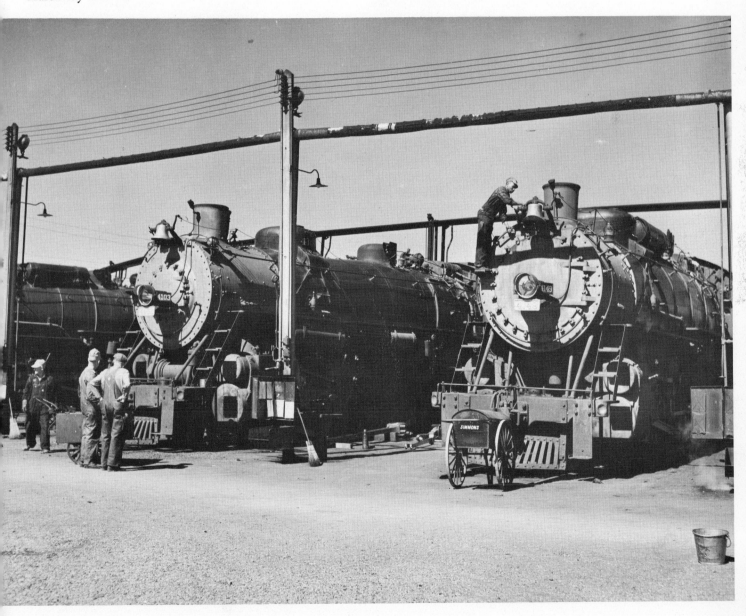

A head-on view of the Frisco's Heavy Mikado type No. 4114 reveals the classic proportions of this numerous tribe of dual purpose locomotives. In the foreground are two of the tools of the roundhouse worker's trade, a flue brush and an engine jack. Airhoses draped over the pilot and a chain come-along hanging from the runningboard steps indicate repairs in progress. The 4114's "coonskin" numberplate was another Frisco trademark.

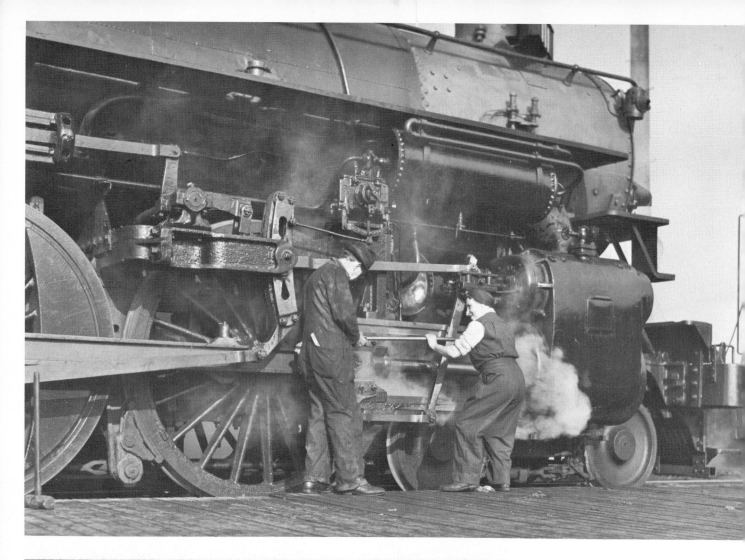

These two photos, although separated in location by nearly 3000 miles, are included to show that not all the women employed by the railroads during the War were relegated to menial chores. The sturdy lass in the safety glasses and bandana is helping to overhaul the valve gear of a Pennsy locomotive at Pitcairn Yard on a June night in 1943. A continent away, on the Southern Pacific ready tracks at San Francisco, her counterpart is adjusting crosshead bolts on a light Pacific assigned to the commuter pool on the Peninsula line to San Jose. (OWI Photos: top, Marjory Collins; lower, Ann Rosener)

The camera of Andreus Finenger captured these studies (*above and following page*) of two Utah Copper Company mallets as they work under the wires dragging carloads of ore up out of the huge open pit mine at Bingham Canyon in November, 1942. Electrified trackage is rare in western railroading except in settings such as this where the trains are frequent and runs are short. Apparently war-time conditions have delayed the retirement of these steamers by cutting off the production of new juice jacks. On mining pikes the distinction between engineer and fireman is not as rigid as it is on the common carriers and the men often spell each other. No doubt this accounts for the obvious seniority of the lantern-jawed gentleman peering down from No. 108's left-hand seat box.

34

Chicago Union Station, 1943

One of the most logical places to start a documentary on wartime railroading would naturally be the largest passenger station close at hand. To Chicago-based photographer Delano that meant the massive and incredibly busy Union Station on Canal Street. Here one could witness the arrivals and departures of the most aristocratic name trains as well as obscure locals and accommodations, identify some of the newest steam and Diesel passenger engines and, above all, mingle with the tremendous throngs of wartime travelers, servicemen, their dependents, commuters, defense workers, all of them contending with the normal stresses of travel compounded and aggravated by continual shortages and delays of near-crisis proportions.

Surprisingly, the traveling public bore up reasonably well and those who can recall bringing empty suitcases on all trips merely for the sake of guaranteeing themselves some kind of seat also remember an amazing cameraderie and sociability that developed among the suffering masses which did much to ease the burdens and frustrations of long hours spent in preposterously overcrowded coaches. Perhaps this singular phenomenon can be attributed to the tremendous anxiety that bore down inexorably on a people locked in a struggle that still seemed decidedly uphill with the enemy dealing out shrewd blows and giving ground at painfully heavy cost.

Whatever it was, people struck up conversations and acquaintances, helped each other as best they could, exchanged snapshots of relatives in uniform serving in exotic and sometimes highly dangerous places, confided fears, sorrows, hopes, and generally carried on in a manner as unthink-

able to the alienated traveling public of the Depression era as it would later become to the increasingly privatistic postwar generations. Somehow, the easing of formal reserve seemed to relieve strains and render more bearable the general discomfort of the times.

There could be no mitigation of all the problems of wartime travel, however, and a good many people permanently put off by the vagaries of the Office of Defense Transportation and the general neglect of the railroads would never again travel by train once peace returned.

To those born too late to share in the human drama of these massive migrations, a detailed portrait of this great station is an eye-opener of another sort for Chicago was the terminus of many of the famous pioneer Diesel streamliners associated with the bold new trends of the 1930s. The Burlington's "shovel nosed" *Zephyrs,* custom designed E units, and a host of other innovative equipment, novelty and glamor long since worn off, were undergoing the acid test of grueling service at a time when the normal temperamental antics of prototypes would have been little short of disastrous. Like the public they served, these relatively untried newcomers drew upon unsuspected reserves of strength and stamina to run up impressive records of performance and availability. They paid their way.

Finally, there remained at the bedrock of American railroading the old reliables of internal expansion. Chicago Union Station played host to Pennsy's legendary K-4 Pacifics, giant duplex drive speedsters, streamlined and steam-styled power of all descriptions and persuasions. It was emphatically no place for the unobservant!

35

In his first series of pictures taken at Union Station in November, 1942, Delano captured the departure of an Alton Pacific with a St. Louis-bound express and the emergence of a Burlington E-5 from the cavernous loading platforms running under Chicago's Main Post Office to the station concourse. Although General Motors instituted rigid standardization of its passenger power with the introduction of the E series, the Burlington insisted on stainless steel fluting, skirts over the trucks, and a pair of false grilles flanking the headlight. These last items were inspired by a desire to retain some link with the "shovel nosed" *Zephyrs* that first inaugurated streamlined internal combustion passenger power on the Q. It's obvious that the steamer's firemen aren't worried about the city's smoke inspectors spying on them this day!

37

The crush of wartime train travel is vividly evoked in this shot of people crowding onto the boarding platform on a Sunday evening in February, 1943. Leaves and passes are due to expire shortly and the need for speed and punctuality is as pressing as the demand for space aboard the trains. Under such conditions there were many instances when schedules could not be met to the exact specifications listed in the timetable but the railroads did their best and on-time performance kept up surprisingly well. Ridership at this point in time is very nearly triple the normal totals experienced in peacetime.

modifications, chiefly to its front end, which earned it the nickname "Funny Face." In 1941 it was converted to a B unit and teamed with a standard E series A unit. This two-unit combination was carried on the Alton's roster as passenger engine No. 50 and it is in this guise that we see it here. Eventually the B unit was reconverted back to an autonomous locomotive and ran for many years in Chicago - Joliet commuter service. Providentially saved from the scrap pile in 1960 it now rests in the National Museum of Transport in St. Louis.

The Baltimore and Ohio's Diesel passenger locomotive No. 50 has just pulled into Union Station with the *Alton Limited* after an epic battle with the midwestern elements, whose grimness is amply attested to by the spattered and begrimed condition of the lead unit's light grey paintwork. The early days of Diesel operations saw few lashups as peculiar as this specimen. The B unit is, in fact, a particularly potent celebrity. Originally purchased in 1935 it was the first passenger Diesel to run on the B & O and the only custom built Dilworth designed "boxcar" the road ever owned. After two years of hard service, No. 50 was sent to the Alton and went through a number of

Also to be found in the murk at the end of the trainshed is one of the Burlington's stainless steel *Zephyrs*. The prototype of these trains was first put into service in 1935 and promptly gave rise to a fleet of look-alikes that ran practically everywhere on the Q's system. Through constant upgradings of successive models, ever-increasing levels of performance and dependability were attained and the *Zephyrs* enjoyed a good reputation with the public. Unfortunately, these trains with their customized power units and homogenous lightweight rolling stock were not to be the real wave of the future. This was, by 1943, markedly veering towards standardized multiple unit motive power that hauled mixed consists of light and heavyweight stock. This pattern was visually less pleasing but operationally more flexible.

Clouds of smoke and steam discouraged passengers from wandering down to the far end of the platforms whenever a Pennsy K-4 arrived with a train so the railroad men had it all to themselves. Here, a goggled engineer just in from Ft. Wayne talks things over with the car inspector. That worthy, whose badge of office is the long-handled hammer hung in the loop of his overhalls, is a vital member of the railroading community. A skilled "car knocker" can detect loose nuts, cracked wheels, and all manner of lesser flaws simply by listening to the ring of his hammer against steel running gear.

At the other end of the platforms, where the outbound power gathered, occasional rays of sunlight penetrated to illuminate the faces of the various subspecies of the Iron Horse. The Burlington's motor unit No. 9906, the *Denver Zephyr*, is seen here flanked by a Pennsylvania K-4 whose dented and cinder-grimed boiler jacket compares most unfavorably with the stainless steel of the Diesel unit. No. 9906, which also carried the name *Silver King*, had two Winton V-12 Diesels and, together with its B unit, *Silver Queen*, totaled 1800 horsepower.

The Pennsylvania's T-1 No. 6110, seen here emerging from the depths of Union Station on a January day in 1943 is a genuine war baby. This duplex-drive monster was designed to be the steam counterpart of the superlative GG-1 electrics, matching their performance and eliminating the wasteful doubleheading of K-4 Pacifics on the *Broadway Limited* and other major passenger trains west of Harrisburg. When this picture was made, only two, No. 6110 and a sister, No. 6111, had been built before the War Production Board had forced a halt to all further construction on the grounds that scarce materials and labor could not be expended on locomotives that were experimental and unproven. Consequently, the two T-1s carried on alone for three years in continuous hard service during which they appeared to distinguish themselves, particularly in terms of sustained high speed performance and endurance. It was only later, after a fleet had been built, that the wisdom of the WPB's policy became evident. High maintenance costs of the Poppet valve system and excessive slipperyness combined to make them, on balance, a colossal failure. No hint of impending disgrace can be detected here though, only the majestic overture of a mighty symphony of steam and steel!

While a track repair gang stands respectfully aside, a pair of Pennsylvania Railroad K-4 Pacifics start a typically heavy wartime passenger consist out of Chicago Union Station on a bitter February day in 1943. Pennsy passenger trains running out of Chicago were often double-headed during the inclement months, the extra power staying with the train all the way to New York.

This fine study of an engine picking her way through an ice-slicked maze of crossovers was made from the overpass above the south entrance of Union Station. The tower, partially hidden by the steam, housed the CTC board that controlled the approaches to the trainshed.

The myriads of track at Union Station were managed by a modern automated interlocking console where men noted the comings and goings of all manner of trains as colored lights flitting across the control panel. Delano was amazed that these men rarely bothered to glance out their windows for a look at the actual trains that they were guiding through the crossovers.

Proviso Yard

■■■

While there was much to be seen and learned in a metropolitan depot like Chicago Union Station, the real drama of workaday railroading was best glimpsed in the sprawling freight yards that laced Chicago's metropolitan area with a vast network of steel rails. Preeminent among these was the Chicago & North Western's mammoth facility at Proviso, widely acknowledged to be the largest classification complex in the world. Proviso, in the winter of 1942-1943 had everything from battered old switching and transfer locomotives to the very latest Diesel terminal facilities servicing a variegated fleet of power assigned to the limiteds which the North Western operated jointly with the Union Pacific and Southern Pacific over the original transcontinental main line.

Here also one found a vast pool of freight motive power dominated by the huge H class Northerns, locomotives so huge in weight and bulk that they were barred from all but the most heavily built and generously proportioned trackage the railroad owned. Their special province was the line from Chicago to Omaha over which flowed the vast interchange traffic destined for California, Oregon, and Washington. Lesser engines, "Zulu" 2-8-0s and J class Mikados supplemented the Hs on transcontinental runs and covered the routes extending north into Wisconsin and south to the coalfields of Southern Illinois. These were relatively light engines for a class I railroad in 1943 and lighter still were the antique Atlantics, Ten Wheelers, and Consolidations that meandered over branch lines dotted with stock pens and grain elevators which contributed many carloadings annually and an unmistakable granger image to their owner's corporate identity.

Also to be found in the engine terminals and servicing facilities at Proviso were passenger locomotives of considerable reputation. E class Pacifics ran commuters out of Northwestern Station until they became so decrepit that their crews took to calling them "Old Soaks" and passengers regaled each other with jokes and horror stories about their wayward habit of shedding quasivital parts along the right of way. Occasionally, one even caught sight of an olive green shrouded E-4 class 4-6-4 spotted at the coal dock between trips on the *Corn King Limited*. These Hudsons were almost as massive as the Hs and likewise were limited to the transcontinental route subject, not unnaturally, to many, many pages of limitations and special restrictions in the operating timetables.

All in all, Proviso was a teeming, bustling terminus on America's Main Stem. Winter's snows and icy vistas only added to the drama with scenes sharply contrasting the patterns of dark rails on white powder and clouds of condensed steam with the black engine smoke of hard-worked motive power. Delano's camera records not only these themes but also something of the extreme rigor of operating a steam locomotive in cold weather. Thawing frozen air pumps, cleaning dirty fires, and contending with the general discomfort of being simultaneously roasted on one side and chilled on the other as the arctic winds whipped through open-backed cabs hung with tattered storm curtains. Under these conditions railroading lost a good deal of its superficial glamour. What remained was the image of a tough and demanding vocation and a rugged band of men and machines.

45

Considering the responsibilities he shouldered and the size of the facility he controlled, the General Yardmaster's office at Proviso was a spartan and singularly unimpressive place. On the wall behind the desk is a map of the vast interchange network of the Chicago Terminal District which, on the North Western was operated as a separate division in its own right. Its territory takes in the Chicago Area from Wilmette to Gary on the lake shore and extends westward past Joliet. Within this area, the North Western and a host of other carriers and belt lines ran an operation of bewildering magnitude and complexity that facilitated thousands of train movements a day.

A view from the west tower of the Chicago & North Western's Proviso Yard reveals a detailed panorama of big-time railroading in and around Chicago. In the foreground, two sections of an eastbound freight enter the maze of classification leads. In the distance ready tracks full of simmering locomotives and waiting cabooses testify to the ceaseless round of comings and goings that typify a busy terminal. A close look at some of those unusually spartan buggies without cupolas or bay windows would seem to indicate that they belong to the Indiana Harbor Belt Railroad and are used in transfer service throughout the Chicago Area.

As a cut of empties from the stockyards pulls into the classification yard, two outbound engines, one of them a J class Mike showing white flags for an extra movement, are waiting to depart. Agricultural products figured greatly in the North Western's scheme of things. Indeed, during the Depression when all other business on the road, ore, manufactured goods, and passenger traffic, fell by an average of 78%, produce, grain, and stock remained relatively strong and kept the North Western from total corporate collapse until the War pushed all traffic to new record high levels.

Here, we're looking across the yard instead of down it. Proviso contained 59 parallel classification tracks exclusive of main lines and service facilities.

(*Overleaf*) This shot was taken from one of the overpasses that punctuate Proviso along its length. In 1942 the yard held 230 miles of track and occupied a space five miles long by a half mile wide. It could hold 26,000 freight cars and was divided into nine separate jurisdictions, each with its own yardmaster working under the direction of a General Yardmaster. The center of operations was fully thirteen miles west of downtown Chicago.

The North Western was never considered to be a very interesting railroad from the point of view of motive power enthusiasts. Most of its freight moved behind engines of no special size or distinction. An exception to this rule were the H class Northerns, hulking behemoths with outside bearings on the leading truck wheels and a unique banjo frame arrangement that supported the firebox over the trailing truck. The thirty-five Hs were the largest engines operating out of Proviso and played a vital role in the road's efforts to keep abreast of wartime traffic. Delivered in 1929, most of the Hs had been extensively shopped in 1940 or 1941 when they received Timken roller bearings on all axles. They also began to have their old spoked drivers gradually replaced with Boxpok centered examples and No. 3032 is about halfway through this process with four of the newer type in place. She is shown waiting to depart for Clinton, Iowa with a long freight on a bitter December day in 1942.

The hump at Proviso was an example of the latest thinking in the lexicon of that famous, or infamous, institution of American railroading. The ascending grade is a long graceful curve that allows the locomotive to shove a lengthy cut of cars along at a steady walking pace while an operative at the crest releases them in predetermined sequence to flow smoothly downhill into the classification tracks. The locomotive in this picture is doubtless one of the two 0-10-2s converted from a pair of Santa Fe types especially for hump service at Proviso. They were numbered 491 and 492 and were originally built in 1917.

The heaviest switchers in use at Proviso, with the exception of two 0-10-2s on the hump, were the M-4 class 0-8-0s of which No. 2642, seen here backing through a turnout, is an excellent example. Although somewhat short in the boiler, these engines were hulking brutes quite capable of taking on transfer assignments or even an occasional mainline haul. Their total engine weight almost equaled that of a large Z class Consolidation, 231,000 lbs. versus the Z's 243,500, but the M-4s weight was all on the drivers and no Z could match that total.

This car of inedible vegetable oils is apparently bound for a track not fully equipped with mechanical retarders so a car rider with a hickory brake club is on hand to insure a reasonably soft arrival at her destination.

54

A portrait of M-4 No. 2637 standing shoulder to shoulder with a J class Mike gives some idea of the size of these massive 0-8-0s, an effect further enhanced by the stubby smokestack and the headlight mounted above center on the smokebox door. No. 2519 is carrying green flags, perhaps indicating that the M-4 will be following her out onto the road as a second section.

M-4 No. 2640 is hustling out of a classification lead with a string of reefers in tow. The exhaust steam billowing out from under the tender indicates that the booster is at work as she begins a short run that will end in the produce district yards some ten miles distant. Around Chicago it was not uncommon for switch locomotives to have tender boosters to help improve road performance for transfer runs.

Adjacent to the classification portion of every large yard are myriads of engine servicing tracks. Here the ground suddenly changes to a filthy shade of black that is a compound of ash and cinders soaked in grease and oil. This area is one of the most fascinating parts of any terminal complex for here the locomotives congregate between runs. Fires are cleaned, coal and water replenished, inspections carried out and light repairs made. An alert observer can often spot the pampered aristocrats and celebrities of the motive power establishment in a candid setting hobnobbing with the commonality. In this case a mighty olive green-flanked Hudson, No. 4009, is sharing a spot under the coal dock with an obscure sister from the commuter pool. No. 1654 is a typical E class Pacific built in 1922.

An M-4 looms out of the enfolding darkness as three switchmen wait to
ride her to their workplaces farther down the yard. Delano was much
impressed by the spectacular photogenic qualities of nighttime action
at Proviso but experienced a certain amount of apprehension prowling
about between the sidings and cuts of cars with nothing underfoot but ice
and hard frozen snow. *(Jack Delano Collection)*

No doubt the most grim and forlorn part of the service area is the ashpit where engines came to have their fires cleaned. As coal burns on the grates of a locomotive, the ash and solid residue are supposed to fall through the slots to the tracks thus making room for a new bed of fresh fuel. Unfortunately, not all the waste does make it through the grate and eventually a mass of ash and rock-sized chunks of "clinker" builds up, blocking the passage of air from below and inhibiting combustion in the firebox. The only remedy is to run the engine over the ashpit and either rake the stuff out with a hook or blast it loose with a compressed air hose. While not one of the most glamorous aspects of steam railroading, this work is vital and locomotives of all ranks and conditions are subjected to the ministrations of the "puddler" and his assistant at some point in their working day.

Two locomotives loom out of the murk as they await reassignment to road service. The brazier in the foreground is as much for their benefit as it is for the roundhouse employees. By keeping the interior temperature above freezing, many problems with frozen pipes and brake shoes are avoided. *(Jack Delano Collection)*

Winter sunlight filters through the windows of a Chicago & North Western roundhouse illuminating the grimy smokeboxes of a pair of old-timers enjoying a respite from the battle they have waged against the mid-continental elements since before the advent of massive-scale world conflict. Three decades earlier these engines had rolled out of the erector's shops into a world of Gibson Girls, nickle beer and dime novels. After having witnessed the first Great Adventure, they served faithfully through prosperity and depression and are now spinning out their final years hauling humble locals and servicing thrice-weekly branch lines.

The North Western's class R-1 Ten Wheelers were a large and venerable tribe. Their tall stacks, slant cylinders, and odd driver spacing made them rarities on a Class I railroad by the 1940s but their design was sound and they could still do useful work. No. 938 was Baldwin built about 1905.

In the dark, steamy interior of the roundhouse, men as well as engines are reduced to shadowy half-phantoms by the brilliant contrast between exterior light and interior darkness. *(Jack Delano Collection)*

65

Although rarely as tidy and well organized as the big boards governing train crew assignments, the Engine Dispatcher's call board was the nerve center of the roundhouse. Here, chalked up on the blistered time-worn blackboard, is the result of a hectic and intricate battle of wits as the Engine Dispatcher strove to provide suitable power for an endless succession of trains, second sections, extras, and transfer runs from among the all too limited stable of power based on his terminal. The men reading the board are charged with the task of readying the locomotives thus selected for the road, remedying any faults or deficiencies in the process. When pressed, almost any of them could tell some gaudy tales of desperate battles and dubious expedients needed to patch up some ailing hog for its date with Second Number such-and-such at 11:46 a.m. The prefix "W" in front of some of these train numbers indicates that they are Wisconsin Division runs. All other power dispatched from this roundhouse will run in the Terminal District or over the Galena Division.

66

Every well equipped roundhouse has at least one repair pit where men can safely move about under the locomotives to service axles, springs, wedges, and other hidden parts that are critical to the life of an engine. Welders like these had an especially busy time with the big Northerns which were in the habit of developing cracks in their frames. When the war was over, the railroad corrected this fault by an extensive rebuilding program that replaced the odd banjo frame system of the original design with a more orthodox integral casting. In the winter of 1942, however, they were simply patched up as best they could be and sent back to the ready tracks.

Cold weather has produced many memorable scenes to delight the lovers of steam but for the men who pull the throttles and stoke the fireboxes it can be pure misery. Consolidation No. 1800, originally a road engine now downgraded to switching chores, has been stored out of doors overnight and has acquired heavy beards of frost on her brake hangers and two thoroughly frozen air pumps. Too old and worn out to warrant refined and delicate treatment, her compressors, dented jackets testifying to past abuse, are being thawed by the simple expedient of jamming oil-soaked cotton waste in their crannies and setting the mess alight. It is obvious that there is scant regard for the principles of good engine grooming where this hog is concerned!

As Mikados went, the North Western's J class were thoroughly unremarkable representatives of the type. Like most other C & NW power, they made up for their lack of distinction by their ubiquitousness and it seemed as though there must have been literally hundreds of them. In fact there were about 200 in all and they formed the road's basic freight power pool. These photos show three Js moving out of the yards at various times with Clinton-bound tonnage. The journal oil is stiff and cold and there is plenty of dirty smoke erupting from the stacks. Note particularly the hot cinders raining down on J-S No. 2587's cab roof.

(*Overleaf*) Somewhat closer to downtown Chicago is the 40th Street Yard with its Diesel engine servicing facilities. A veritable profusion of internal combustion power is on hand this crisp December day undergoing turnaround grooming and adjustments between calls for the crack overland runs that originated at North Western Station many blocks farther east. In addition to one of the *City of Denver* locomotives, which shows up prominently on account of its massive grille, there are several E-3 units in attendance including a *City of Los Angeles* locomotive which entered service in 1939 and a sister assigned to the *Twin Cities 400*. *Twin Cities* power can be distinguished from the Overland pool by the dark green paint on the upper sides and roofs of the units.

Much of the freight forwarded west to Proviso came from the New York Central Railroad via the Indiana Harbor Belt Line which formed a connecting link between the eastern railroad's terminals in East Chicago/Hammond and the western carrier's facilities at Blue Island, Proviso, Bensonville, and other West Chicago suburbs. Here an IHB transfer run with New York Central interchange tonnage pulls into the classification leads.

The dubious look on this fireman's face hardly needs to be translated. It is obvious that those storm curtains are no substitute for a proper all-weather cab!

The bitter cold of a December night is condensing the normally invisible exhaust of this M-4 into a pillar of steam as her crew waits for a clear block before setting out for Clinton, Iowa. In the crisis-ridden environment of this second winter of the war, a husky 0-8-0 might well expect to draw some road assignments but one can be sure that the crew will earn their pay this night mauling the low-wheeled rough-riding switcher over the road with nothing but the puny storm curtain visible at the top of the gangway between them and the cold winds whipping down from the Canadian Arctic.

No operation as large as Proviso can function for long without some mishaps. With thousands of cars being humped or flat switched every day, it is only natural that a few should become headaches for the claims department. This boxcar stored on the bad order track appears to have been lifted off its wheels and jackknifed. One wonders if the trucks she is riding on are part of her original outfit as they appear to have suffered almost as much as the car body. Journal lids are missing and baulks of timber wedged in where the springs ought to be.

77

A close look at the *City of Denver* motor as she emerges from her steam cleaning gives us a dramatic head-on view of a species of Diesel power fully as individualistic and distinctive as the Burlington's *Zephyrs*. Three bulbous nosed CD locomotives arranged in A-B-B sequence were built by Pullman in 1936. They ran over the property of the Chicago and North Western and the Union Pacific and were jointly owned by both roads. The three units making up each locomotive totaled 3600 horsepower and were powered by Winton Diesels and General Electric traction motors. They had heavy duty rubber bumpers mounted above their pilots and a retractable coupler is concealed under that icicle "beard". The twin unit drawn up alongside appears to be *City of Portland*.

"One Hundred Miles ... Shall Constitute a Day's Work"

■■

One hundred miles is a unit of measure in American railroading which has all the significance of a divinely ordained mystical incantation. Ever since the operating brotherhoods had wrung their first great concession from the ranks of management establishing that eight hours on duty or one hundred miles traveled constituted a full day's work and that no train crewman could be kept on duty for more than sixteen consecutive hours, the standard administrative unit, the division, had been fixed at more or less the century mark.

A consequence of this arrangement was the development of certain towns, otherwise obscure and unfavored, as major rail centers complete with shops, roundhouses, railroad hotels, YMCAs and administrative offices. Another development was the settling of the railroader's working life, assuming he had enough seniority to bid himself off the infamous extra board, into a reasonably predictable routine. Regular hours, a permanent route and fixed days off replaced the old practice of "doubling" which once saddled men with continuous duty for as long as 48 hours at a stretch.

Whether or not they held permanent assignments, the rituals of the day's work were much the same for trainmen all across the nation. Picking up waybills and orders, comparing watches, inspecting locomotives and running gear, meeting opposing trains, relaying hand signals, and perhaps indulging in a savory bit of "caboose cookery" were the very essence of a job that quickly became a way of life for its practitioners.

The following photos are a record of one such working day in the life of a Chicago and North Western freight crew assigned to the double tracked, high density Galena Division which constituted the first leg of the road's main line west. Clinton, Iowa, 120 miles across the flat Northern Illinois prairie is the extent of their run, although their train, delivered to an Iowa Division crew, will continue on to Omaha and interchange with the Union Pacific. Clinton was also the end of the run for the Big H class Northern which the Engine Dispatcher had thoughtfully provided.

Number 3014 and her sisters were welcome power on just about any Galena Division train in those days. Nicknamed "Zeppelins" by their crews, they were among the earliest Northerns built and, although their specifications were marginally exceeded by the Rock Island 5100 class and the Norfolk and Western's mighty Js, the Hs were never decisively outclassed. Their massive, hulking aspect, especially when viewed from head on, was somewhat misleading and belied the fact that they rode on 76″ drivers and were most successful dual-purpose machines. In 1943 they looked like they would last forever. Alas, Number 3014's date with the scrap merchant was just eleven years into the future and that after a thorough rebuilding in 1948 had corrected her few original design flaws.

The real charm of this sequence of photos lies not with the locomotive but rather with the train crewmen themselves. Associates of long standing, they perform their familiar tasks with an economy of motion and a quiet competence that imparts the unmistakable imprint of authenticity which was, more than almost any other factor, the true hallmark of government documentary photography.

The crew of time freight No. 251, scheduled to leave Chicago for Clinton at 11:00 a.m. are gathered in front of their locomotive discussing their impending run and waiting for a highball from the tower. The conductor is the gentleman on the right with the waybills shoved into his coat pocket. The engineer in the middle and two brakemen complete the group. Only the fireman, already busy on the deck with routine housekeeping chores, is absent.

Two activities as old as railroading itself are taking water and comparing times. The regulation railroad watches these men carry are timepieces of extraordinary accuracy and dependability. They are never set or adjusted on a daily basis and therefore any differences must be noted and remembered by the men themselves since only the company watch inspector may move the hands. Once a month each watch is checked and the gain or loss of minutes and seconds over the previous thirty days is noted. Any watch that varies more than two minutes from the previous month's setting must be either repaired or replaced. The reason for such stringent standards is that time in railroading translates into distance and a train one minute off schedule is often a mile or more away from where it should be at a given point in time. The crew of Northern No. 3009 are preparing for a run to Clinton, Iowa over the Galena Division which was the only line out of Chicago on the North Western that had the generous clearances and reinforced bridges necessary to accommodate an H.

With departure time fast approaching, the engineer and conductor compare times. Notice that No. 3014 has only one pair of Boxpok drivers at this stage of her career.

Unlike the passenger terminals where highballs are given by cab signals and lights, the freight ready tracks are devoid of complicated devices and the departure signal is relayed by hand from tower or yard office to head brakeman and thence to the engineer. In the background is one of the North Western's J-4 class Berkshires. Two years older than the Hs these Berks were virtually the only other more or less modern heavy freight power on the system.

While preparations to get underway are completed at the head end of No. 251, the rear brakeman has little to do but hang up his markers and wait for the train to whistle off. On an adjacent ready track his counterpart on the preceding section makes a quick sprint for the platform steps of his rapidly accelerating buggy.

Before joining the main line in the flat farm country west of Proviso No. 251 is obliged to wait on a feeder line under flag protection while an overland passenger train powered by an E-4 Hudson thunders past on its way to Omaha and the Coast.

The pot-bellied stove was once a universal and highly functional artifact of American railroading. Depots, coaches, yard offices, switch shanties, all were warmed in the winter by these cast-iron gnomes with their built-up tin chimneys and flat tops. Like many ingenious devices of yesteryear, they could function in a dual capacity as both heater and cookstove. A steel rail around the top makes this one particularly convenient for toasting sandwiches and simmering a pot of coffee. By 1942 pot-bellied stoves had long since been phased out of use on passenger equipment because of the fire hazard they posed in the event of a wreck but the freight crews still used them faithfully and would until the end of steam locomotion cut off their coal supply. This picture makes the reasons for such loyalty obvious.

A conductor's caboose is his castle! While his long, slow freight rattles towards Clinton, the skipper busies himself with his waybills while the rear brakeman gazes off into the middle distance. Since these men hold a regular run they have the advantage of a permanently assigned crummy fully equipped with a coffee pot, a barometer, a purloined sign fraudulently advertising the presence of a dining car, and a few choice specimens of what was delicately referred to in those innocent days as "leg art". Who could ask for a more pleasant home away from home?

87

Once the train has been dropped off in the yards at Clinton, the conductor and his rear brakemen hitch a short ride in the cab of a locomotive to the yard office where the Skipper will turn in his waybills before checking into his rooming house for a mandatory 8-hour layover. No. 3016 and her crew continue on to the roundhouse where the engine will be quickly serviced and dispatched east again within a few hours.

Delano's return trip from Clinton to Chicago was made in the cab of No. 3016 whose engineer is seen here lubricating the bell of his locomotive before departing with a long string of reefers containing West Coast perishables. As the train moves eastward daylight slowly replaces the freezing predawn darkness. The engineer has made his throttle and reverse lever settings and has his ear cocked to listen for the even, unlabored drumming of smokestack and cylinder exhaust that will tell him that he has achieved the right balance of forces to ensure smooth, economical performance.

It is now full daylight and No. 3016 has stopped to fill her coal bunker at a chute built over the main line at Nelson, Illinois. Our eastbound drag is running on the left-hand main, the very opposite of standard practice on most American railroads but quite appropriate on the North Western which perpetuated the habit of left-handed operation instituted by its original English management.

A day's work did not always mean a trip over the road to the next division point or a spell of duty in the yards. Some of the hardest working railroaders were the shopmen and mechanics who worked in shifts in the North Western's repair facility at 40th Street doing heavy repair work and major overhauls. Here we see the huge erecting bay where ten locomotives, not counting the integral cast underframe in the foreground, are in different stages of undress. Locomotives of various rank, from 0-6-0 switchers to J-4 class Berkshire No. 2808 can be identified. (*Jack Delano Collection*)

This welder is standing inside the smokebox of an engine which has just received a new set of flues. The front end of a locomotive boiler is the scene of much critical activity in the process of generating drawbar horsepower. Hot gasses from the firebox drawn through the flues by the draft caused by exhaust steam from the cylinders are blasted up the stack with each stroke of the pistons. Great quantities of soot and cinders, some to be voided and some to collect in a heap on the bottom of the chamber, were the bane of roundhouse employees who had to crawl through a circular door just behind the headlight to remove the stuff by the shovelful. Two dry pipes supplying steam to the cylinders curve downwards on each side.

The steam locomotive was always one of technology's cruder energy converters and nowhere was this crudity more evident than in the smokebox. The behavior of the gasses swirling within was never well understood by designers but the inability of the exhaust steam to punch through the smoke and effectively clear the chamber with each piston stroke was one of the great limiting factors retarding the efficiency of internal expansion motive power. After the war European railroads introduced the Geisel ejector which substantially improved efficiency in the front end by more precisely metering the flow of steam through the exhaust nozzles but that came too late to do the North Western's elderly hogs any good.

93

Open butterfly doors reveal the grimy faces of two boilermakers hard at work renewing arch brick in the firebox of a J class Mike. Although this work is no picnic, those men at least have the advantage of working on a cold engine. Roundhouse crewmen were occasionally obliged to venture into the firebox when it was hot to make quick repairs or caulk leaky flues on engines carded for fast turnaround. In those cases, boards were laid on the bed of coals, the worker was wrapped in wet sacking, and a helper stood by with a hose to douse the unfortunate soul when he reemerged. Nobody tarried to milk these jobs! The idea was to get in, do the work, and get out again fast.

It's dirty work indeed checking the flues and overhauling the superheater tubes of an H class Northern. The open smokebox gives us a rare and interesting view of the Worthington type S feedwater heater and its steam pipe connections. Unlike the Elesco types, Worthingtons appeared above the boiler shell only as a very modest square structure but, like the proverbial iceberg, that's not all there was to it by any means. (*Jack Delano Collection*)

The numbers stenciled on the smokebox of this locomotive indicate that class three repairs are in progress. Class three overhauls stop short of a complete disassembly of the entire locomotive but do involve the stripping and renewing of all exposed moving parts and the application of a fresh coat of asbestos boiler lagging.

An Indiana Harbor Belt Album

As the nation's principal rail center, Chicago probably played host to a wider variety of switching and transfer operations than any other metropolitan region. Just about every major railroad that served the Windy City and its attendant industrial complexes either carried on its own extensive terminal activity or owned at least part interest in a system that specialized in sorting and delivering cars to a multitude of customers of every possible description.

The equipment needed for heavy transfer activity was, like the men who traditionally hired out as car riders in the hump yards, of various and often dubious origins. Demoted road engines, often hand-me-downs from some parent road, ran out their final milages within the vast industrial wasteland of the Chicago Switching Limits. Inordinately large 0-8-0 shunters, complete with tender boosters and oversized drivers, paddled up and down the long hump grades, classified cars in "flat" yards, and even took their turns on transfer runs long enough to approximate the extent of a normal division on a full-fledged trunk line. On assignments such as this, no train was complete without a worn, splintered caboose to serve as headquarters for a conductor whose responsibilities included not only complicated switching problems but also the ticklish task of threading his train through a complex network of leased and shared trackage integrating it into the traffic of half a dozen class one carriers. It was no job for the faint of heart!

The Indiana Harbor Belt Railroad was just this kind of operation. It listed a mere 126 route miles but its milage in sidings, spurs, and yards ran into the thousands. It was run as a subsidiary of the New York Central which owned most of the stock but it preserved its own corporate identity and character. IHBs transfer locomotives were mainly Mikes identical to the Central's own H 5s right down to the massive Elesco feedwater heaters that overhung their grimy smokeboxes while its 100 class switchers were reputed to be the most powerful 0-8-0s in existence, exerting 89,000 lbs. tractive effort with the booster working.

Despite its individualism and partisan ownership, the IHB actually functioned as part of a smoothly coordinated network of belt lines that facilitated Chicago's role as a gateway between East and West and as a major industrial center in its own right. This smoothness unfortunately, had not always been the rule. Up until 1912 Chicago transfer operations were so chaotic and confused that delayed cars jammed all the major yards, especially in the winter months, and several bypass routes utilizing the Peoria gateway and Lake Michigan car ferries had to be established. The Belt Operating Agreement of that year did much to alleviate these problems by establishing uniform switching rates, granting important access and trackage rights to various roads and generally replacing the spirit of cutthroat competition that had prevailed since the 1880s among the belt lines and their overlords. Consequently, World War II found Chicago a highly rationalized rail center through which traffic was routed and expedited in a manner befitting a true Arsenal of Democracy.

All of this managerial harmony and apparent civilization could not alter the fact that transfer railroading in the Chicago area in mid-winter 1943 was pretty much a dog's life for the operating personnel. Hand firing, continual shunting, and heavy traffic put the head-end crews through their paces while the conductors and brakemen cursed the bitter cold and chilling winds as they tended switches, set out cars, and performed numerous inspections looking for burst air hoses, broken draft gear, stray track skates and a host of other potential hazards. Their trips may have seemed short to mainline railroaders but transfer runs were generally round trips with constant delays, caboose hops, and the need to share congested, often borrowed trackage. Twelve hours on duty at a stretch was not uncommon and the crew worked hard for the whole time with no high speed running to eat up the miles, no restful waits in the hole, and plenty of complicated operating rules and procedures to keep track of. A transfer crew railroaded the hard way and came off duty bone weary.

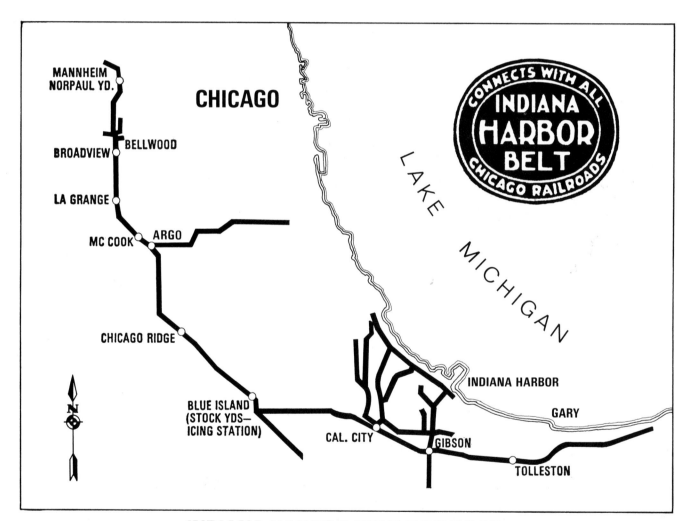

INDIANA HARBOR BELT RAILROAD

98

The IHB was a strictly utilitarian operation that spent very little time and energy grooming its locomotives, especially in winter. Switcher No. 307, shown here delivering loads to a feed mill in Blue Island, has accumulated so much grime that even her number plate is thickly coated and all but illegible. The robust 0-8-0 is typical of much belt line power. Her lack of truck wheels made her handy in the yards while her oversized drivers gave her the speed and endurance needed for long transfer runs with full sized trains in tow.

Another Chicago Area subsidiary of the New York Central was the Michigan Central whose engine No. 257 is seen pulling past the IHB freight station at Hammond with a transfer caboose in tow. The 257 is sporting a snowplow pilot, a contrivance common in the western mountains of Colorado and California but decidedly rare east of the Rockies.

A good deal of IHB running was done on borrowed tracks. Here we see a doughty 0-8-0 rattling over the Michigan Central's iron at Hammond, Indiana with a long string of cars destined for interchange in one of the major West Chicago yards.

Indiana Harbor Belt's Class H-5v Mikado No. 421 has just arrived at Proviso to pick up a string of cars for redistribution to other points around the Chicago Area. The 400 series engines, outshopped by Lima in 1925, were patterned directly on similar power built for the parent New York Central System. They proved very effective and durable motive power and lasted until the end of steam on both roads.

Revenue tonnage was not the only thing that rode the hump on the Indiana Harbor Belt. Here, a waycar complete with markers and a brakeman ready to "club down" in the time honored fashion of an old-time roustabout car rider, coasts downhill towards its waiting train. At one time most of the hump switching in the Chicago area was done this way and a rough business it was! Riders rode each car to its destination in the yard applying the brakes by hand with the aid of hickory clubs like the one shown above. When a car lacked brakes, the rider found out only when he tried to apply them and that was much too late. Unless a "skate boy" could manage to throw a wedge shaped track skate under the wheels the runaway would either derail in the switches or pile into the cars at the end of its run. By 1943 the practice was being phased out by the introduction of mechanical retarders but the skillful use of the brake club was not yet a lost art.

A borrowed New York Central locomotive is taking water at the IHB's eastern terminus in Hammond, Indiana. How many persons can view a scene like this without secretly hoping that the tallowpot will somehow manage to run the tank over? Even on a frigid day in February, the prospect of instant Niagara Falls is an enticing one!

...ing covered IHB switching operations in the Hammond
...a on foot for a week in early January, 1943, photog-
...her Delano finally wrangled an opportunity to accom-
...y a train crew through a routine working day. His trip
...ted at 11:30 am in Norpaul Yard, the IHB's western
...minus located at Franklin Park about ten minutes' run
...n Proviso. The first job of the day was for Engine
...1381, a borrowed New York Central H-5n class
...ado to pick up a caboose from the ready track. Transfer
...mmies tended to be rudimentary vehicles often devoid
...cupolas and other amenities. Many were conversions,
...heavy outside underframe of the one nearest the
...ne in this picture indicating that it was once a loco-
...ive tender.

Rattling down the IHB's main line from Norpaul Yard to
Proviso we overtake an inbound transfer movement powered by sister H-5n Mike No. 264 wearing the Company's
own monogram. Our orders call for us to pick up a train
for delivery to Blue Island, there to pick up another train,
routing instructions to come later.

103

The tracks leading into Proviso Yard are busy on this bitter winter day. No. 1381 has dropped the caboose and is backing down to the ready track to pick up the cut of cars destined for Blue Island. Two C&NW Z class 2-8-0s, one powering an outbound drag, can be seen in the background.

While the engine crew collects the train, the conductor and rear brakeman confer with the C&NW Yardmaster, comparing tally sheets of cars and ladings. Crewmen on the IHB spent a good deal of time negotiating with the men of other railroads, a job that called for a certain amount of tact and diplomacy as well as letter perfect paperwork!

While waiting for the highball to depart for Blue Island, the engine crew trades jibes and gossip with a North Western switch-man.

It's always an eerie sensation to look out the rear door of a caboose and see another train drifting down the track towards you. Perhaps the realization that a rear-end collision, even at low speed, can easily reduce a crummy to kindling and spread jack-knifed cars all over the landscape lends suspense and some degree of apprehension to encounters of the sort recorded here. Still, the bunching up of trains waiting for signals to clear is a common part of railroading and the crew of Delano's train is doubtless reassured by the vigilant aspect of the following section's head-end crew, both of whom can be seen leaning far out of their respective cab windows carefully gauging speed and distance remaining. The locomotive is a 400 series 2-8-2.

107

Arriving at Blue Island, the first train was quickly dropped off and the second, consisting mainly of a consignment of meat bound for the New York market, was picked up. Orders came through routing it to the Erie Railroad via Hammond and specifying a 6:00 pm delivery so that it would reach New York the next morning after a fast overnight haul. As the train pulled out of the yard, the sun made a brief appearance backlighting steam and engine exhaust while the rear-end crew made the usual running inspection before catching the caboose.

Following morning delivery in New York seemed a bit ambitious and sure enough, it was. A derailment on the IHB main line through Calumet City has diverted our train to an alternate route through the Chesapeake and Ohio and Wabash Yards and put us hopelessly behind schedule in reaching Hammond. Feeling our way gingerly along foreign iron, we encounter a three-way meet with a short cut of cars in charge of another IHB Mike and a long string of tank cars, part of a Baltimore and Ohio freight and a very potent symbol of the times. With coastal shipping menaced by U-boats lurking off the Atlantic and Gulf ports, much of the burden of moving heating oil and fuels fell to the railroads. By September, 1942, they were delivering 800,000 bbls *daily* which amounted to 70% of the nation's total consumption. During the summer of 1943, a crash program of pipeline construction managed to lift some of the burden but the railroads continued to haul significant quantities of oil until well after V-J Day.

A fireman's job on the IHB was very much a vital occupation for most of the large switchers on the system were "hand bombers" and required plenty of patient toil with scoop and slash bar to keep them going. As a consequence, IHB engine crews were notorious for their tendency to "appropriate" any decent scoops lying about on the property of the many roads they visited in the course of a day's transfer run. When not occupied on the deck in the everlasting battle involved in keeping steam pressure up to an acceptable level, IHB firemen could enjoy a splendid view of the industrial debris and general detritus of the industrial backlots of Hammond, Calumet City, and Chicago.

An early winter twilight is settling over the yards at Hammond and the day trick crews are coming in to tie up for the night. Switch lanterns and markers are already glowing brightly and the square windows of the yard offices and trainmen's shanties are sharply outlined and hint of the warmth to be found within. The low clouds hold their own promise—more snow to come.

An additional set of orders, delivered at Hammond, directs our crew to return light to Norpaul Yard. This means retracing the day's journey, a task that will consume five more hours and put them into their home terminal at 11:45 pm. Even so they are lucky. Forty or fifty loads dropped on them by the dispatcher would take much longer to deliver and stretch their on-duty time to the sixteen-hour limit. Now nothing remains for the rear-end crew to do but hustle some coal into the pot-bellied stove and settle back for a ride punctuated only by a lunch stop at Blue Island where the rear brakeman gives the fireman a hand by topping off the tender. Obviously jurisdictional niceties were not an overriding concern among the IHB crews.

Midwestern Miscellany

In covering rail activity in the Chicago Area Delano quite naturally placed particular emphasis on those roads where he had become reasonably well known and could return often without having to reintroduce himself each time. He did, however, visit several other railroads in addition to his old favorites, the Chicago and North Western and the Indiana Harbor Belt. These included the Illinois Central, the Burlington, the Milwaukee Road at Bensonville, and the Pennsylvania at Cleveland, Ohio. Here is a sampling of the photographs he took at these diverse places and properties.

On the fringes of Corwith Yard an Alton 2 8-0 in transfer service delivers a string of military trucks to the Santa Fe for shipment to the West Coast. Note the homebuilt yard caboose behind No. 2988's tank. Apparently consisting of a shack built on an old flatcar, it can certainly be said to afford plenty of platform space!

A trip to the ore docks at Cleveland resulted in this shot of Pennsy Decapod No. 4444 (left) lugging a cut of hoppers filled with Missabi rust out of a siding on a gray afternoon in May, 1943. The ponderous I-1s "Hippos," rough riding, conservatively engineered brute freight haulers, were among the last of their wheel arrangement to be mass produced for any American railroad and it has been argued that they were obsolete from the very day they left the Baldwin works in 1922. Nevertheless, they were a useful and long-lived breed and ran on the Pennsylvania's rails until the very end of steam operations.

Bensenville, Illinois, just west of Chicago on the C M St. P & P's line to the Twin Cities, was a good place to go to see the best Milwaukee Road power during the war years. Whether it be an F-7 class Hudson charging past the order board at Tower B 17 with one of the several daily *Hiawathas* or a dual purpose S-2 class Northern clearing the yards with a long string of high cars, the spectacle was sure to be rewarding. The S-2s were among the latest and most advanced steam locomotives in service in 1943. Their all-weather cabs, solid steel pilots, Boxpok drivers and Timken roller bearings were representative of the best practices in the field of internal expansion power. Near sisters of the Baldwin-built 200 series were at work on several other roads at this time, including the Northern Pacific and the Rio Grande.

The Milwaukee Road used its extensive yards at Bensenville as a major terminal for freight consigned to the Chicago area from the Twin Cities and the Pacific Northwest. From here the trains were broken down and cars distributed to destinations in Greater Chicago via transfer runs and switching movements. Perhaps the light engine and old-fashioned caboose in the foreground are starting out on just such an endeavor.

A venerable Milwaukee Road Consolidation (below) gets underway for Chicago with a Bensenville transfer run.

Cow and calf units were a rare sight in 1943 when Delano made this sequence of Nos. 9205 and 9251 in South Chicago. In fact, there were only five in existence and all of them were owned by the Illinois Central and used in hump and transfer service in the Chicago area. The first group of three, of which No. 9205 and her slug unit are members, was built by EMD in 1940. A second pair, similar but with more powerful Diesels and traction motors, was built in 1941 to complete the quintet and No. 9251 was one of this latter group. War Production Board rulings suspended further construction of transfer power for the duration of the conflict and it was not until 1946 that more of these units were built.

Another hardworking addition to the nation's total of internal combustion units in service by 1942 was the Rock Island's brand new Diesel yard goat No. 701. Apparently the Rock Island crews thought well enough of the little shifter to nickname her "Billy Boy", a monikker that will last at least until her next wipe down at the roundhouse.

119

Number 3618's sister "Dec" No. 3616 is seen dropping back down the hump on her way to pick up yet another cut to be boosted over the summit. The short steep grade on this "pimple" is not on par with the best humps of that day which called for a much longer and more gradual ascending grade. This measure eliminated much of the slamming and jolting involved in stopping and starting cars on a short steep incline, allowing the locomotive to keep traffic flowing in a smooth and orderly progression.

Modern day purists who object to the fact that many of today's fan trip locomotives are obliged to tote an "unauthentic" auxiliary tender are encouraged to study closely this view of Illinois Central's Mountain type No. 2530 which sported an extra tank in 1942. The I.C. resorted to this device in an effort to speed up long distance passenger and freight schedules. Other Central engines thus outfitted included the 2700 series 2-10-2s.

The Illinois Central retained a significant number of 2-10-0s in service during the 1940s and found them to be reasonably efficient locomotives for hump and transfer service in their South Chicago yard. Here, No. 3618 takes on coal and sand at the massive fueling facility which served scores of the Central's locomotives over the years.

In late afternoon twilight a Santa Fe caboose departs Corwith Yard with markers glowing brightly. Caboose markers of that era were multicolored, showing red to the rear and green or amber to the sides. *(Jack Delano Collection)*

A Journey Begins: Chicago to Kansas City

Early in March of 1943 Photographer Delano wound up his coverage of railroading in the Chicago area and prepared to set out for the Pacific Coast as a guest of the Santa Fe Railroad. The principal reason for selecting this road was that it was just about the only main line on which he could traverse the Heartland of America and reach California entirely under one corporate banner. Critics might conceivably grumble that other transcontinental routes, such as the Union Pacific's line across Sherman Summit or the Rio Grande's passage through the Rockies, would have been much more scenic, featured a greater variety of motive power, and generally allowed for a more representative treatment of Western Railroading. Unfortunately, choice of these routes would have multiplied the amount of negotiation, paperwork, and general red tape involved in dealing with three managements instead of just one. Since the spirit of the moment was to work with all possible speed and efficiency, the convenience of going "Santa Fe all the way" proved decisive.

This is not to say that the Santa Fe's operation was anything less than mainline transcontinental railroading at its best! Its first 449 route miles, from Chicago to Kansas City, was double tracked high iron that carried an endless parade of crack passenger limiteds, long fruit and produce blocks, and heavy drags of merchandise and munitions. It featured mammoth bridges spanning the Mississippi and Missouri Rivers, a busy helper district to lift trains out of the Illinois River Bottoms at Chillicothe, and the sprawling classifying yards at Corwith and Argentine to serve as terminals.

Originally completed as the Chicago, California, and Santa Fe Railway in 1888, the four subdivisions of the Illinois and Missouri Divisions represented the last step in a series of corporate acquisitions and construction projects which transformed the Santa Fe from a cattle and wheat hauling prairie pike into a common carrier of continental dimensions.

Despite its strategic significance, the Illinois Division proved to be something of an orphan from the railfan's point of view. The corporate image promoted by the Santa Fe's publicity people heavily overemphasized the Spanish and Indian heritage of the Southwest at the expense of the rolling plains of Illinois and Missouri. The great steam locomotives of the Texas and Northern types, motive power that every knowledgeable rail buff associates with "John Santa Fe" rarely ventured this far east and even the early Diesels were seldom found here with the exception of wholly unrepresentative Alco DL 109 units and a handful of switchers. The engines most frequently found on these rails were fleets of husky Mikados dating from the early twenties and some old Santa Fe types and Consolidations, the latter acquired when the A T & S F took over the old Orient Line.

The following photographs will establish, however, that relative obscurity does not necessarily equal unimportance. This least publicized and most uncharacteristic portion of the Santa Fe's far-flung empire was a busy place in 1943 and a good introduction to mainline railroading of the highest order.

(*overleaf*) The date is March 6, 1943 and Winter is still very much in evidence as our journey begins at the Santa Fe's Corwith Yard. Fresh snowfall the previous night has necessitated a good deal of shovel work to clear the switch points and insure that they will not freeze up solid with "blue ice" on subsequent evenings.

This shot of two of Corwith's long-suffering switchmen riding the footboards of an early Baldwin Diesel switcher is of interest mainly because of the rare oval grille sported by the sturdy little yard goat. During the late 1930s the Santa Fe invested heavily in Diesel switchers from a variety of manufacturers. The Baldwin Diesels were most in keeping with Company traditions, however, as this builder was the Santa Fe's favorite and almost exclusive purveyor of steam motive power. No. 2202 represents an attempt to maintain and continue a long and fruitful corporate alliance that is actually doomed to collapse in the near future. Baldwin Diesel power was soundly designed and tailored to the specifications of each customer but the way of the future was already evident in the standardized mass-produced units built by General Motors at its La Grange Works. Unthinkable as it was in 1943, there would come a day when there would be no more Baldwins of any sort on order for the Santa Fe.

A proverb says that a journey of a thousand miles must begin with a single step. When traveling by rail, the beginning of a trip is more definitely announced by an engineer and his conductor comparing times and running orders.

126

The two long blasts of the whistle indicate that the impatient hogger is ready for a clear block signal. In this case, the engineer of No. 3266, a heavy coal burning 2-8-2, is signaling for clearance to depart Corwith with the photographer's first train. The husky Mike is to be our head-end power as far as Ft. Madison, Iowa, two subdivisions and one crew change away.

The Santa Fe was so proud of its extended trackage that it made a promotional montage out of a simplified map of the system. Jack Delano's impending trip over a goodly portion of this territory made his encounter with a Company owned reefer in Corwith Yard something of a prophetic event.

Chillicothe, Illinois, is a change point for crews and cabooses. As practiced by the Santa Fe, this maneuver was both fast and efficient. First, the new crummy, No. 1743, and its crew were picked up by a yard goat and taken to the train. The old caboose, No. 1860 is removed and shunted to a siding. The switcher then returns to the train and couples the new buggy to it. A new crew takes over the locomotive, which is usually run over several subdivisions, and the train continues on its way.

There is just time to snap off a quick shot as a local passenger train thunders past our caboose. The Chicago-bound accommodation with its old style tourist coaches is representative of an ancient and honorable mode of travel in the railroad era for it was trains like this one and not the name limiteds that carried the bulk of the passenger traffic.

The Chillicothe helper pool also contained a few of the old 900 class 2-10-2s. These engines were members of the original group of tandem compound ten-coupled heavy freight hogs that first carried the name of the railroad into locomotive nomenclature as the Santa Fe type. Long since converted to single expansion and oil firing they have been bumped from the more demanding grades out West and sent here to run out their final mileage boosting drags out of the Illinois River valley.

Besides being a crew change point, Chillicothe is also a helper terminal. The two husky Mikados in the foreground are shown under the shadow of a huge coal dock taking on oil fuel and sand. No. 3185 is a Baldwin product of 1918 while the 4000 is the prototype of the last series of 2-8-2s ever built for the Santa Fe. A total of 115 locomotives of this class were added to the roster between 1921, when No. 4000 arrived, and 1927. This made them the largest single class of 2-8-2s on the property. They and their earlier sisters of the 3160 class were the Santa Fe's basic road power between Chicago and the mountains of New Mexico where ten-coupled power took over for the Raton and Abo Pass grades.

For the climb to higher ground west of Chillicothe, our drag has acquired a heavy duty pusher in the form of Mikado No. 3286. Although coupled into the rear of the steel underframed caboose, she is not connected to the train's air line. For this reason, when the summit is attained, she can be let go "on the fly" simply by lifting the coupling lever on the crummy's deck beam. The helper then drops back while the train continues on with no time lost.

With the grade behind us, the pin is pulled and No. 3286 drops back a suitable distance. Green flags on the smokebox indicate that it will run as a second section for a short distance to the next crossover and then return back downgrade on the eastbound main. The Santa Fe's operating personnel were most proficient at these nonstop evolutions and carried them out with smooth efficiency.

The coming of darkness heralds the end of Delano's first day on the road. Meanwhile the conductor, finished with the mundane task of tallying waybills, studies a copy of the Employees Timetable with the aid of an electric light. A more traditional coal oil lamp is bracketed to the wall as a standby in case the newfangled generator fails.

Delano climbed to the top of the coal dock to get this panorama of the Santa Fe's engine servicing facilities and repair shops at Ft. Madison (Shopton), Iowa.

The locomotive status boards at the Shopton roundhouse held a gold mine of priceless information in the days of steam. The Passenger Work Record Board is dominated by 3400 class Pacifics and 3460 series Hudsons but the eighth entry, carded for train No. 20 involves Diesel units 1 and 1A, the railroad's first passenger Diesels purchased in 1936 and recently rebuilt at the Streator shops. Two gasoline-powered "doodlebugs", Motors 176 and 186, are also on the list. Over on the right, the Locomotive Inspection Data Board reveals a freight lineup that included a few Prairies (1800 class) and a much larger contingent of 3160 series medium sized 2-8-2s. The complex testing and record keeping detailed here was vitally necessary in order to reduce the threat of boiler explosions and to keep the Interstate Commerce Commission's inspectors pacified.

These two Santa Fe Co. photos show Diesel units 1 and 1A as they looked in 1936 and again in 1943 after extensive rebuilding at Streator in 1942. The renumbering evidenced in these pictures apparently took place after Delano passed through Ft. Madison. (*Both photos, Santa Fe Railway*)

All those reams of technical data on the status boards ultimately translate into the tangible form of locomotives such as these awaiting road assignment at Shopton Roundhouse.

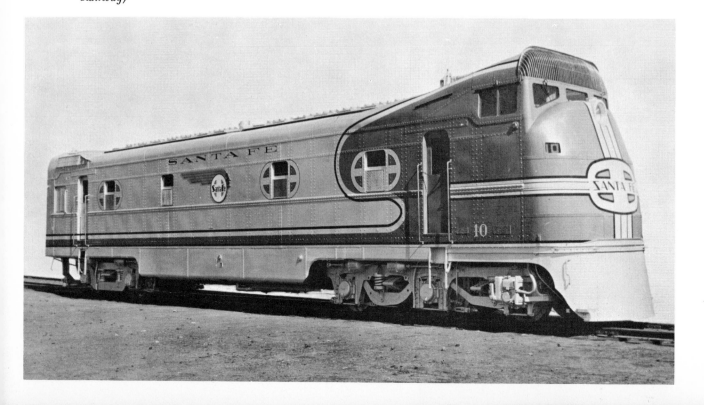

Marceline, Missouri was a typical crew change point on the Missouri Division. The bleak yards contained little more than some empty ready tracks and engine servicing facilities. The east- and westbound mains swing around to the right and left facilitating the movement of trains that are going on through without stopping.

The Marceline Dispatcher's Office is a blend of the old and the new. A telegraph key shares space with the new CTC board that governs the main lines as they circle the yards. At this point, we are about midway between Ft. Madison and Kansas City.

The Santa Fe crosses the Missouri River on a high bridge located about twelve miles east of Kansas City at Sibley. While his train was waiting on the eastern approach for an opposing train to clear, Delano made this shot of the Santa Fe's only Alco Diesel road units, two DL 109s styled by Otto Kuhler and delivered to the road in 1941. Numbered 50 and 50A, the pair were first assigned to the Chicago-Los Angeles *Super Chief*. This transcontinental grind on a twice-weekly schedule proved a little too tough for the Alcos and by 1943 they had been reassigned to lesser trains plying between Chicago and Kansas City. An earlier broadside view of this locomotive taken by a company photographer at some mission-styled station in the Southwest gives us a clear view of the lean rangey look of these low-slung units. Within this compact layout 2000 horsepower could be generated in each unit making them even more powerful than the bulkier E units which were their contemporaries.

Photo — Santa Fe Railway

Once the bridge is clear, our freight moves out over the Missouri River. In early March the river is at a low stage but within a month or so the melting of snow on the Northern Plains and mountains will flood all of the dry land in the foreground. When this happens, the Santa Fe's tracks, which now seem excessively high over the water will not appear to be as comfortably removed from harm's way as they do here.

Looking back at the bridge after the crossing it can be seen that although it accommodates only one train at a time it is not necessarily a single track operation. Westbound trains ride the left outside and right inside tracks while eastbound traffic uses the right outside and left inside rails. Crossovers at either end of the span obviate the need to stop and line up switches so trains are not unduly delayed while the Company enjoys the economies of a bridge that is much cheaper to build and maintain than an ordinary doubletracked span would be.

141

A light dusting of snow has covered Kansas City's Argentine Yard as Delano's train pulls in. At this point he is one night and two days out of Chicago.

Central Kansas and Oklahoma

■■■

Any serious study of the Santa Fe Railroad must sooner or later explore its relationship with the State of Kansas. Occupying the exact geographic center of the continental United States, Kansas is both the birthplace and the unchallenged fiefdom of the Santa Fe. In addition, the largest metropolis of the Central Plains region, Kansas City, is also the site of the system's most extensive and important facility, the gigantic Argentine Yard which extends for some ten miles or more along the banks of the Kaw River just west of the Metropolitan Area.

The role of Kansas City and Argentine Yard in the far-flung operations of the Santa Fe can best be understood in comparison with Baltimore's importance to the B & O or Pittsburgh's significance in the affairs of the Pennsy. Although many other roads served Kansas City, the Santa Fe was clearly predominant, moving 7000 cars a day through its own facilities and interchanging another 1500 to 1600 with the Union Pacific, Frisco, Burlington, and Rock Island systems, among others.

Nevertheless, for all its complexity, Kansas City was just the beginning. From Argentine's western yard limits a four-track main line extended to Holliday where the lines diverged, one following the Kaw (Kansas) River straight west to Topeka while the principal freight route, now doubletracked, curved southwest to Emporia and Newton Junction. Passenger trains usually traveled on the Topeka line which rejoined the main stem at Hutchinson thus keeping at least one of the road's namesake towns firmly in the center of things. The other two, Atchison and Santa Fe, had been largely bypassed somewhere in the evolutionary process that had transformed the

bucolic prairie stock hauler of the era of trail driving and wide open towns into the corporate giant of the war years.

Topeka maintained its importance in the Santa Fe's scheme of things not only by housing the usual collection of classification tracks, roundhouses, and terminal facilities, but also the road's main car building shops and an extensive complex of locomotive repair facilities. These were virtually working around the clock to construct, repair, or recondition rolling stock and locomotives of all kinds in order to meet the insatiable demand for cars and motive power spawned by wartime traffic expansion.

Operations in Kansas proceeded at a brisker pace and traffic became significantly heavier than it had been on the eastern divisions. Huge Northern types made their appearance on passenger runs and there was even an occasional F T unit on freight which served to boost drag speeds into the seventies while varnish consists rolled at the ninety mark or above. Bypasses and alternative routing over parallel lines allowed the Santa Fe to dispatch trains as though it possessed a three- or four-track main line running the length of the state. Not content to furnish mere background for the passage of an endless stream of bridge traffic, Kansas also generated considerable on-line revenue to add to the staggering totals of tonnage carried across its plains and river bottoms.

Here then, deep in its own heartland, is where the spectacle of the Santa Fe at war achieves its true uniqueness and individuality. From Kansas City on, Jack Delano will be moving through country not shared but *dominated* by the "Comp'ny" and stamped with its own particular image.

143

Among the more nondescript cars that flooded Argentine, it was possible to spot cargos that were obviously destined for the War. Here we see a line of M-4 Sherman tanks on flatcars. It is interesting to note the extent to which the railroads have gone to safeguard this cargo. Canvas shrouds protect against the elements, wooden chocks prevent shifting, and placards specify careful handling and no humping. It all seems designed for something more delicate than a tank.

144

We are standing at the control console with the operator at Turner Interlocking, located at the west end of Argentine Yard. Here, trains originating in Kansas City are directed onto the four-track main line that extends to Holliday where the passenger route diverges from the principal freight line and heads for Topeka. Keeping his eyes firmly on the colored lights of his console, the towerman rarely glimpses the trains he guides through the maze of crossovers. A typical representative of these "movements" would be Extra 3167 West, a mixed freight drag seen from the tower stairway as it clatters past on its way to Central Kansas.

From the point of view of the motive power enthusiast, the Santa Fe's most representative locomotives are first encountered working the lines west of Kansas City. This included Diesels as well as steamers and doubtless one of the most valuable entries on the engine dispatcher's list was F T unit No. 103. This four-unit freight Diesel was among the first of its kind to arrive on the property back in 1941 (numbering of freight Diesels started with 100 in the War Years). She is seen here emerging from her stall in the roundhouse with white flags already in place for an extra movement west. Our next glimpse finds her snaking a long drag out of the ready tracks in the vicinity of Turner Interlocking on her way to Emporia.

Before leaving Kansas City, Delano took a side trip to Topeka to visit the complex of shops where heavy repairs and overhauls were done on the locomotives and rolling stock assigned to the Santa Fe's central divisions. In this view the Topeka yards seem somewhat less congested than those at Argentine but this is only because much of the activity goes on indoors in the car galleries and erecting bays. Yet, there are no less than six plumes of steam visible, each representing a diminutive six-wheeled switcher, bustling about the yard.

Topeka was the location of the Santa Fe's principal car shops and here we see a typically dreary collection of victims of the fundamental roughness of railroad technology. These cars on the bad order track were probably smashed in yard shifting and derailments out on the road. Significant improvements in the methods of train dispatching and widespread use of sophisticated signaling equipment had largely eliminated the frequent collisions between trains that characterized railroading in the World War I era but there was little that could be done to prevent equipment failure from taking some toll on the hard worked and deliberately overloaded rolling stock plying the rails in 1943.

The War Years produced a tremendous demand for rolling stock of all kinds just when the production of new freight and passenger equipment was curtailed by even more urgent priorities elsewhere. Faced with this situation, the railroads assigned a great deal of importance to repairing and reinstating wrecked and retired equipment. Since the need was so great expense was no object and sometimes an old car was refurbished at a cost that exceeded its replacement value. Still, the restoring of old cars did not require the securing of War Production Board approval and Government permits. Cars could also be built in the Company's own shops whenever repair work did not keep the crews fully occupied. In all, the Santa Fe reinstated a total of 5,675 previously retired freight cars between 1940 and 1946; 17,025 new cars were acquired, most of them before the end of 1942. However, 18,165 had to be retired during the same time so the net gain was only 4,535. Since the volume of freight carried tripled during the war it is easy to see why every possible derelict was salvaged.

In this shot, some of this important work was taking place out-of-doors due to overcrowded conditions in the shops. Note the double ended G.E. switcher over on the caboose track at the right.

An 80-ton Whiting overhead crane has capacity to spare for lifting the stripped down boiler and underframe of Mikado No. 3261 off the jacks and blocks down at the boilermaker's end of the Topeka shops. Further up the long bay the mechanics and their helpers are waiting to undertake the ticklish job of wheeling the venerable hog. As the boiler is slowly lowered, shopmen stand beside each major bearing block to ensure that the wheels have been spaced for a proper fit. Once the locomotive is down on her drivers, these men will reassemble her rods, valve gear, steam lines, and numerous other fixtures. With a fresh coat of black paint the boys at her home terminal will be hard put to recognize the clanking, wheezing, semi-cripple with worn bearings and broken staybolts that they sent over a few weeks earlier.

While traversing the short section of four-track main line just west of Kansas City we get a glimpse of a real aristocrat. No. 3771 is a super 4-8-4 with 80" drivers. When delivered new in 1938 she was considered one of the most powerful and efficient Northerns ever built, easily capable of running an overland limited straight through to Los Angeles, 1,788 miles via Amarillo, without more than routine service stops. After a brief layover at the Redondo Junction Roundhouse in L.A., the 3771 will be ready to start east again. This kind of endurance and availability was a standard feature of the Santa Fe's Northerns which established records few other modern steam locomotives have ever duplicated. Proof of No. 3771's transcontinental operations can be seen in the form of the blackout hood on her headlight, a mandatory piece of equipment for all locomotives operating near the Pacific Coast in those days.

Not everyone got to work out-of-doors at Topeka. Air hoses and electrical leads indicate that this boilermaker peering out the butterfly doors of a freight locomotive is busy with heavy repairs in the firebox. A soot begrimed cap and a pair of goggles attest to the grimy conditions he has to contend with in this line of work.

Exciting and dramatic as the appearance of No. 3771 was, we are still in Mikado territory watching from the caboose cupola as 47 cars of mixed merchandise rumble west behind yet another of that sturdy breed. On the eastbound main line, trains are flashing by periodically and a good deal of doubleheading is encountered. This was caused, in large measure by the Santa Fe's attempts to get additional ton miles out of its regularly-scheduled trains by adding more cars than usual. This doubleheader encountered near Emporia is somewhat unusual in that the locomotives are identical sisters. The usual Santa Fe practice was to team a lighter engine up to run as helper while a heavy modern locomotive held the main assignment.

Emporia Junction was a busy place on the Eastern Division lines. Here, the passenger route via Topeka rejoined the main stem while another line branched off for Southeastern Kansas. There was also a crossing to guard and orders to be delivered to such passing trains as required them.

Pulling into the yards at Wellington, we catch a glimpse of two very awkward and vital waybill entries in the form of a sixteen-inch naval rifle and an enormous cannister destined for the Kaiser Steel plant at Fontana, California. Both of these items, which seem to dwarf the several flatcars needed to accommodate them, are examples of the specialized challenges that the railroads met and overcame in the process of delivering arms, munitions, and implements of war of every possible description. A statistical study by the Southern Pacific Railroad concluded that American railroads moved eight tons of cargo for every casualty inflicted on the enemy.

Mikado No. 4096 is typical of Wellington-based power. A 4000 class engine, she has probably spent her entire life working beneath the shadows of enormous grain elevators and wheeling drag freight across the level Kansas Prairie.

Wellington is a major division headquarters in South Central Kansas with Santa Fe iron converging on it from four directions. The engine crew's callboard reflects the variety of assignments and the number of important routes that are serviced by the locomotives and crews stabled here. Notice that the lineup of road engines working the Middle Division is made up exclusively of 3160 and 4000 class Mikes.

Here's a wartime innovation that will have a definite application at a later date. These M-1 light tanks, shown here being unloaded at some Army camp in Central Kansas, are rolling off a ramp that is one of the humble forerunners of the hundreds of piggyback terminals that are a prominent feature of modern railroading. (*Santa Fe Railway photo*)

Leaving its train drawn up before the station platform at Harper, our locomotive runs for the water plug to top off the tank for the next leg of the trip.

The next one hundred miles of our journey, as far as Waynoka, Oklahoma, will be covered in a Division Superintendent's business car cut in just behind the tender of Mike No. 4097, shown here getting a few drops of oil on her bell yoke. Green flags on the smokebox indicate that there will be a following section as we race down the long tangents of arrow-straight iron extending in a southwesterly direction towards the Texas Panhandle.

Engine No. 4097 pauses for routine servicing at Kiowa, Kansas. The black locomotive crouching in the shadow of a white grain elevator is a striking evocation of the mood and spirit of the Great Plains. Scenes like this one were often included in the compositions of the great Missourian Thomas Hart Benton, a noted painter and iconographer of the life and culture of the prairies. Indeed, two more potent symbols of this vast breadbasket region could scarcely be imagined. Let no man say that the Santa Fe should not be included among the ranks of the granger roads!

Headlight, number boards, flags, classification lights and markers are the hallmarks of a train movement. When these are mounted in the proper order the consist in between is immaterial. A number is assigned, an entry is made on the Dispatcher's train sheet, and provisions must be made so that the movement can be integrated into the flow of traffic. This rail detector rig, which resembles nothing so much as a wayward city omnibus, is a full-fledged extra, apparently being held for orders under the board at Kiowa, Kansas. Out on the road, her function is to detect potentially hazardous worn spots and flaws in the rails before a break causes an accident. Like many safeguards in railroading, her value can never be measured because her function is preventative. Standards of track maintenance and inspection were high during the War Years, especially when contrasted with today's haphazard practices. One wonders if this little gas buggy was replaced when she wore out and how many damage claims and lives she saved during her career.

After her servicing stop at Kiowa, No. 4097 pulls up to the yard limits at the south end of town to wait out the clock before continuing on her way. For all but a privileged few who hold down first-class passenger assignments, a railroader's life is filled with delays of various durations. Waiting for order boards and block signals to clear, waiting for opposing trains to pass, waiting for new orders in the event of some unforeseen mishap, or merely waiting for time to pass in order to stay within timetable authorizations could take up a good part of the working day. Although both semaphores are showing "clear", a few minutes must elapse before we can continue. The second signal in the middle distance guards the crossing of the Missouri Pacific's line to Hardtner.

When the signal to depart is finally given, the veteran runner assumes the classic pose familiar to small boys the world over during the great age of steam. Within a very few minutes the throttle is notched far enough along the quadrant to fan a brisk breeze through the cab, causing the all-important sheaf of train orders that will govern this day's run to flutter against the clipboard that hangs at the hogger's knee. On the left-hand seatbox, the young fireman keeps his eye on the steam gauge as he adjusts the oil burner control.

Upon arrival at Waynoka, (above right) No. 4097 is spotted alongside the water plug to top off once again before continuing on to Amarillo under the guidance of a new crew. This makes her second crew change of the day in a run that will see her cover two more subdivisions before she ties up at Clovis, New Mexico, over 200 miles further on. Clovis was the farthest west that the Mikes normally traveled. Ten-coupled power in the form of Texas and Santa Fe types was the normal freight power on the western lines.

164

A brief stroll to the engine servicing tracks at Waynoka is rewarded by the sight of two elderly Prairie types, No. 1122 built in 1902, and No. 1843, a product of the vintage year 1907. When originally built, these sprightly 2-6-2s were intended for fast freight and passenger service. Now long past their prime, they have been retained to handle branch line traffic and to run as helpers for overloaded road engines of more modern build. Both of these old-timers were originally designed as compounds. No. 1122 on the Vauclain pattern and No. 1843 as a balanced compound type with two high-pressure cylinders mounted inside between the low-pressure cylinders. This was an efficient design and very popular on the Santa Fe but servicing was a nightmare. Both engines were simpled in the 1920s.

The night trick telegrapher at Waynoka, seen here throwing a switch on his interlocking console, was in charge of a fairly complex and exacting operation. Telegraphers were an interesting and very crucial breed of railroader. Variously known as "brass pounders", "lightning slingers", and a host of other nicknames, their job was to keep the Dispatcher posted as to the progress of all trains working over his district by means of out-of-station (OS) reports and to deliver train orders and other messages to the operating crews. Sometimes, when things were slow in the small hours of the morning, a kindly Distpatcher might let them gossip in morse over the wires or even play checkers on numbered boards but mostly they worked hard and diligently. The responsibility that they carried for the safety of the trains and crews that roared past their bay windows was a heavy one requiring accuracy and meticulous work habits. Even a minor mistake in copying a "31" order could cause an accident that would have every operator on the line frantically examining his conscience and reviewing his actions until the exact cause of the wreck could be found and the responsible party pinpointed.

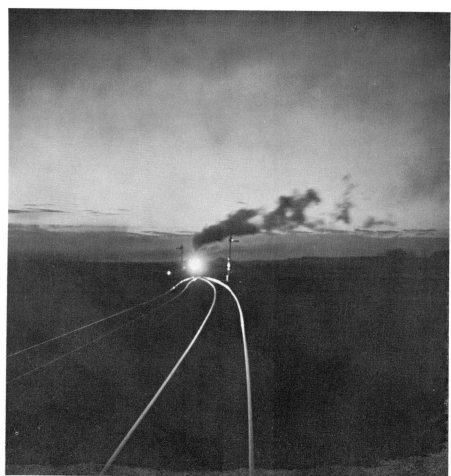

Dawn is just breaking over the eastern horizon near Belva, Oklahoma, as a helper arrives to couple onto our caboose for the stiff climb out of the Cimarron River valley, to Curtis. Some twenty minutes later, at the top of the grade, the helper is cut off "on the fly" and drifts slowly back just as a fast eastbound freight whips past. The whole tableau is captured by the camera in a frozen moment of timeless beauty against the brilliant morning sky.

From Curtis, Oklahoma, to Pampa, Texas, the Santa Fe was single track territory with movements governed by timetable and train orders. Delano's freight has pulled into a siding to let a long passenger train powered by a 3750 class Northern, with a light Pacific running as helper, overtake it. No. 1386 was originally a balanced compound built by Baldwin and simpled in the 1920s. During the last years of steam operations, many of these superannuated Pacifics were relegated to running as helpers and some of them even served as freight power in California's Central Valley where the grades were slight but schedules called for fast running on the fruit blocks and other perishables shipped over the Valley lines.

The Belen Cutoff

■ ■

One disadvantage of traversing the Santa Fe by freight train was that our photographer missed the most scenic part of the entire system, the original main line over Raton Pass. As a general rule, all westbound transcontinental freight left the old line at Ellinor, Kansas and swung south through Wellington and Amarillo to link up with the Belen Cutoff at Clovis. From there, a heavily traveled single tracked line struck west across Central New Mexico, crested the Los Pinos Mountains at 6,730 feet at Abo Pass, and descended abruptly towards the Rio Grande River valley and the town of Belen. A short distance further on, at Dalies, the tracks rejoined the original route for the assault on the Continental Divide.

This more southerly line, completed in 1908, not only gave the Santa Fe a route slightly shorter than the line over Raton but had the added advantage of being 1,100 feet closer to sea level at its highest point. It had a ruling grade of only 66 feet to the mile, comparing most favorably with the 184.8 feet to the mile that obtained in the towering Sangre de Cristos.

Actually, for the first 400 miles, from Ellinor to Clovis, the freight route was something of a speedway with long level tangents that invited engineers to thunder along at seventy or eighty mph with even the heaviest drags. Grain elevators, solitary sentinels of the plains, lined the right of way ready to accept the bountiful harvest of spring and fall, a golden flood that fed over 120,000 carloadings annually to the Santa Fe

alone, requiring three times as many boxcars as the road possessed to move it. Next there was a stretch of double track extending in arrow-straight tangents across the Texas Panhandle, where trains could whip past each other at combined speeds of 150 mph, perhaps the fastest running meets for freight drags on the entire system.

West of Clovis, things became a little more hectic. The sawtooth profile between Clovis, Abo and Belen was a difficult section to operate and tended to create bottlenecks as trains fought their way to the summit from either direction and light engines tried to clear their time while returning downgrade. It is a significant tribute to the superlative 5000 class Texas types that they were rated at 4000 tons westbound and 4800 tons eastbound over this district. All trains required helpers.

To cope with this enormous volume of traffic which often totaled more than thirty separate train movements every 24 hours and included four passenger runs of no particular pedigree, the railroad installed one of its earliest CTC units at Clovis covering 25 miles of particularly congested main line as far as Melrose. Further plans were afoot to establish two more CTC panels, including a mammoth unit sixteen feet long at Mountainair to cover the entire 119 miles of helper territory. When this equipment was ready, around the middle of 1944, the Cutoff's capacity was increased by better than fifty percent and congestion eased considerably. Still, it was and remains a challenging piece of railroad!

A friendly wave to a passing train crew represents more than just a fraternal greeting. Throughout the winter of 1942-43 the Santa Fe, along with other U.S. railroads, had experienced a 30 percent increase in accidents related to equipment failure. Consequently, whenever it was possible crewmen did their opposite numbers on opposing trains the courtesy of looking over their running gear. The casual high sign actually means that no hotboxes, dragging parts, or unsecured freight are visible. The prosaic stance of the other crew can be taken to mean the same.

These two views of a westbound freight *(lower left and below)* departing Amarillo were made from atop one of the several grain elevators that lined the tracks near the Santa Fe's yards. Amarillo is the primate metropolis of the Texas Panhandle and the source of hundreds of carloadings of agricultural products annually.

With sleeves rolled up and a bullhorn slung over his shoulders, the dispatcher at Amarillo directs the flow of traffic over 73 miles of double track between Pampa and Canyon. An ingenious earhorn allows him to receive verbal reports from the various telegraphers scattered along the right of way without the bother of a conventional telephone but he has only his trainsheet to aid his memory in keeping tabs on the scores of train movements which pass through his territory during each day. Although double tracking and block signaling made the Plains Division somewhat easier to manage than was usually the case in western railroading, the responsibilities weighing on this man are awesome and his margin for error is slight.

Once again the familiar green flags bracket the smokestack of a sturdy Mikado bound from Amarillo to Clovis, New Mexico, with one of several sections of a westbound freight. During this period of capacity operations there were few trains to be seen on the road that did not show either white for an extra movement or green for a following section.

Once more in single track territory, our train has pulled into the hole while the conductor picks up new running orders. These are "31" orders which, unlike the "19" order, cannot be picked up on the fly but must be signed for in person by both the engineer and the conductor of the recipient train. Incidentally, the little depot in the background is something of a classic in that it contains within one well-integrated structure all of the essentials of a typical American whistle stop. There is a Railway Express Agency platform, telegraph bay, waiting room, and Western Union relay. Thanks to this facility the tiny hamlet of Black is in full touch with the world.

Our train is stopped (*above*) on the main line near Par-merton, Texas while a superior train uses the passing track to pull around it. The rear brakeman can be seen leaning out of the cupola window waiting to look over the op-posing drag.

Clovis (*left*) is the point on the Belen Cutoff where the Great Plains end and the assault on the Continental Divide begins. Here the 2-8-2s of the 3160 and 4000 classes relinquish their domination of the Santa Fe's freight oper-ations to the larger and more powerful ten-coupled loco-motives of the 3800 and 5000 series. The exact spot chosen for this symbolic changing of the guard is the Clovis roundhouse. In this photo, a massive Santa Fe type is turned on the transfer table while two Mikes linger under the coaling dock in the background. Coaling facilities were

rare but not unknown on the Santa Fe which owned 262 coal burners out of a total fleet of 1500 steam engines. The two main centers of coal-fired operations were the eastern subdivisions between Ft. Madison and Chicago and the various lines in New Mexico, both of which took advantage of plentiful supplies of black diamonds fur-nished by nearby mines.

Stopped by the order board at Texico (*top, left*) on the Texas-New Mexico state line, the engineer of this 3160 Series Mike has left his seatbox to stroll over to the depot and find out what the operator has for him. At the far left of the picture, the caboose of the preceding section can be seen receding into the distance as its train picks up speed again on its way to Clovis.

175

One notable habitué of the C[...] roundhouse was No. 5000, the [...] Texas type to be added to the S[...] Fe's roster discounting an experi[...]tal locomotive of that wheel arr[...]ment improvised from a 3800 [...] 2-10-2 back in 1919. When she [...] first put into service in 1930, the [...] was an immediate success and [...] crews promptly dubbed her "Ma[...] Queen" in honor of her great siz[...] mechanical excellence. Unfortun[...] by the time the railroad was thr[...] testing and analyzing her perform[...] the Depression had begun to c[...] traffic and no further engines [...] ordered until 1938 when eleven [...] sisters were received from Bal[...] No. 5000 never relinquished her [...] however, and could always be [...] tinguished from the 35 other [...] types (numbers 5001 through 5[...] by her large Elesco feedwater [...] er which sat like a crown atop [...] smokebox.

This is the view from the cupola of a caboose tied to the marker's end of train No. 4-43, 86 loads and 6 empties, powered by 2-10-4 No. 5004 and running between Clovis and Belen. The freight in these cars is a random sampling of the diverse categories of goods needed to sustain global war. Mattresses, nails, hospital supplies, airplane parts, trucks, pipe, gasoline, steel, glass, soap, hogs, soybeans, and more for a total of 4,293 tons. This was 293 tons over the normal rating for a Texas type, a serious matter insofar as the roadbed is already gaining altitude at the rate of 32 feet per mile.

A long curving embankment leading to the bridge crossing the Pecos River at Ft. Sumner, New Mexico, affords the photographer a chance to get a clear shot of his entire train.

At the coaling dock and water tank at Yeso 4th 43 is overtaken by No. 5000 at the head of a long extra freight. .

Although not the most glamorous aspect of railroading, track work is of vital importance and much attention was given to the maintenance of the strategic western main lines. A pressing need to replace ties and renew rock ballast along the Santa Fe's right of way near Iden, New Mexico, has resulted in the temporary establishment of a wholly self-sufficient town on wheels complete with water cars, bunkhouses, and a rough-and-ready kitchen. One of the ironies of wartime railroading was that while many women were being hired to work at jobs once thought exclusively within the masculine province, cooking remained a man's job. Watching one of the chefs preparing bread dough by the washtub full for baking in a huge coal fired range one can easily see why. Only a man could have both the strength and stamina necessary to prepare three heavy hot meals a day for dozens of hardworking men *and* the moral authority to see to it that the inevitable grousing about the food did not go beyond a certain point. The emphasis here is on the solid and substantial so the cook's day begins early and ends late.

180

A meet with an eastbound extra at the tiny hamlet of Buchanan finds Delano's train taking a siding to run around the opposing train which holds the main.

182

Fourth No. 43 is swinging into a long curve just west of Vaughn. The high embankment carries the Santa Fe's tracks over those of the Southern Pacific's line from El Paso to Tucumcari. Although the S.P. was, like the Santa Fe, mainly an oil-fired operation, it took advantage of a plentiful supply of New Mexico bituminous and assigned some coal burners to this run which explains the presence of this coaling dock. The locomotives which utilized this facility included not only the 3800 series Mallets but also some borrowed Boston and Maine Berkshires that had come west to ease the power shortage on the strategically vital trunk lines across the deserts. The Santa Fe also had borrowed B & M Berks at work in New Mexico as well as some Norfolk and Western articulateds in helper service over Raton and Glorieta Passes.

Upon pulling into Vaughn, one hundred miles west of Clovis, Delano got a close look at one of the newer Texas types. No. 5006 is part of a group of ten locomotives that arrived on the Santa Fe's property in 1938. These sisters, numbered 5001 through 5010, were equally divided between coal and oil burners and all of them worked on the two subdivisions between Belen and Clovis. In 1944, a second group of these fleet-footed monsters. Nos. 5011-5035, were added to the roster and likewise assigned to the Belen Cutoff. Possessing the tallest drivers of any ten-coupled locomotive and the longest rigid engine bed ever cast, the Texas types combined phenomenal tractive effort with great speed and stamina. In later years, when Diesels bumped them off their mountain runs, they proved most successful in hauling heavy produce blocks at high speeds across the level prairies to Kansas City. No amount of speed or efficiency that these brutes could demonstrate was sufficient to stem the Diesel tide, however, and the twenty-five engines purchased by the Santa Fe in 1944 constituted the last major investment in steam motive power the road was ever to make.

Notice the curious rigs on the cupola of the cabooses in these pictures. The 5000 class engines could haul trains that were so long that the Santa Fe felt constrained to install semaphores atop the crummies so that the rear end crew could communicate with their counterparts on the point without making a mile-long trip over the swaying car tops.

An acute shortage of waycars led the Santa Fe into some rather dubious expedients. This hack *(upper left)* found sitting on the caboose tracks at Vaughn is obviously a converted boxcar. Although lacking in end platforms and cupola, its most questionable feature is its side door, a contrivance so notable as a cause of death and dismemberment among railroaders that crummies so equipped were outlawed in interstate commerce. The Santa Fe put a number of these conversions in service during the war and managed to stay within the law by assigning them to branch line operations and local runs that did not cross state lines and consequently never became subject to Federal regulation. This one was used primarily on the Stanly Branch.

The summit of the long sustained grade that began at Clovis is finally attained near this bleak and lonely depot at Abo, *(left)* New Mexico, elevation 6,730 feet. Here

Delano's train made a triple meet with an opposing drag whose helper can be seen in the distance beyond the order board and a work train powered by an ancient 2-10-2. No. 976 is equipped with one of the unique whale-backed tenders that once belonged to a 2-10-10-2 Mallet. Originally ten in number, these mammoth engines were rebuilt into twenty conventional Santa Fe types after the Santa Fe gave up on articulated power in the early 1920s.

The passenger station at Belen is a busy place this March day in 1943. During peacetime most of the Santa Fe's passenger traffic shunned the cutoff route for the more scenic Raton Pass line. The war has changed all this, however, and there are plenty of troop extras, mail trains, and locals which were enjoying a brief popularity thanks to gasoline rationing. In this picture, no less than three such trains are visible in the vicinity of the brown simulated-adobe depot.

The freight yard at Belen (*left*) is likewise a busy place with a double headed drag and a troop extra waiting on the ready tracks while steam and Diesel switchers sort and classify a wide variety of rolling stock. Belen's yard is not only a division point on the east-west line but also accommodates the passage of considerable traffic on the Santa Fe's Rio Grande Division running between El Paso and Albuquerque. It is situated at one corner of a triangle that is the principal hub of Santa Fe operations in New Mexico.

Isleta, just south of Albuquerque on the Santa Fe, is an important junction for it is here that the Rio Grande Division tracks diverge from the main line to follow the river to El Paso. Meanwhile, the main stem curves away to the right to link up with the Belen Cutoff at Dalies before striking west across the desert to Arizona. With both routes working to capacity, the order stand at Isleta is a busy place and hickory hoops with "19" orders affixed are much in evidence.

Motor No. 119, a gasoline-powered unit with a mechanical transmission, is the first recipient and then it's over to the stand to set the hoops for a freight following the "doodlebug" into Albuquerque. After snaring their respective sets of orders, the train crews will discard the hoops along the right of way to be retrieved by the operator. In the old days, Santa Fe telegraphers often kept dogs specially trained to fetch the discarded hickories. A good "hoop mutt" could often save his master a lot of walking over the years and they were handed down from operator to operator as part of the station's normal establishment.

Here's a reminder that some of the Santa Fe's cherished peacetime standards of excellent passenger service were upheld even in a period of acute world crisis. The *Super Chief,* westbound for Los Angeles, is drawn up before the brown Mission style passenger depot at Albuquerque while her General Motors E-3 units take on fuel from a pair of tank cars conveniently spotted at the end of the brick platfrom. White jacketed porters, along with inspectors and passengers are swarming around the lightweight stain-

less steel cars and one father has even taken his two boys down to the head end to see the Diesels. Albuquerque was a major servicing stop for transcontinental passenger power on the Santa Fe but, while a 3750 class Northern would require at least 20 minutes for greasing, fire cleaning, fuel and water, the sleek EMD units will probably be ready to depart before most of the passengers have time for more than a quick cup of Fred Harvey's coffee — and there'll be no need for a trip to the ash pit!

Overhaul work is going on around the clock at the Santa Fe's Albuquerque shops. No. 3733, a Mountain type passenger engine, is undergoing Class 5 repairs during which some 25,000 parts will be carefully checked, renewed, or replaced with something more up to date. When this process is over, her performance should equal or exceed the records she set when she was fresh from her builders.

One of the most persistent myths about the steam locomotive was that, unlike the diesel, there were no complicated parts to inventory and keep in stock and that whenever a replacement was needed it could be hammered out over an anvil in the blacksmith's shop. This photo, taken in the storage yard of the Albuquerque shops should lay that idea to rest. Modern steam locomotives needed a backup of spares just like any other hardworking mechanical contrivance. Here we can see valve gear linkages, driving axles, suspension springs, mainrods, a stoker screw, and even replacement smokestacks.

A close look at No. 115 as she passes shows that although she is less than two years old she is already showing a few signs of hard use. One of the reservations that trainmen had about the earlier Diesels was the cab arrangements which put them right "up front". Although this made for greater visibility, the crews felt exposed to more danger, especially in the event of grade crossing collisions involving cars and trucks. To assuage these fears GM designers strongly reinforced the nose of the F T units so that the men rode behind a massively buttressed ram designed to deflect wreckage and preserve intact the cab and its occupants. This resulted in the famous "bulldog" snout that was a permanent feature on Electro Motive power up until production of E and F units terminated over a decade later.

Diesels Across the Desert

■■■

From Chicago to Gallup the Santa Fe was emphatically a steam railroad. The few Diesel road engines that operated over the Illinois Division and on the main lines through Kansas only served to prove the general rule. Once the tracks reached Arizona, the picture began to change and on the 459-mile stretch of rugged desert railroading between Winslow and Barstow Diesels were present in considerable force.

The giant FT units with their vermilion and blue "warbonnet" color schemes that dominated the various subdivisions of the Albuquerque Division were part of a fleet of 88 units delivered to the road before the end of 1942 and helped introduce America to the first practical freight Diesels for mainline operation. In fact, the first "covered wagons" employed by the Santa Fe were direct descendants of Electro Motive Division's No. 103, the original demonstrator locomotive that had barnstormed the Santa Fe and other western roads in 1940.

The performance, availability, cleanliness, and simplified servicing of these visitors had made a deep impression on the Santa Fe's management, an impression further strengthened by the statistical readouts furnished by the Company's dynonometer cars and other figures compiled over the toughest portions of the system. For example, fuel costs for Diesels ran $11.61 per ton as opposed to $5.04 per ton of oil fuel, the road's principal propellant. The milage that could be obtained from a ton of fuel oil averaged out to 20.37 systemwide while Diesel fuel yielded 133.13 miles to the ton. When the war came fuel economy for all forms of motive power slipped downwards on account of the general increase in train lengths but the ratio of milage obtained per ton of fuel remained constant. Diesels ran six times as far on fuel that cost only twice as much. The Santa Fe became a convert to Diesel freight power just as it had earlier committed itself to Diesel switchers and passenger engines. Ultimately it became the first railroad in the world to use Diesels simultaneously in all three major phases of railroading, freight, switching, and passenger service.

The crews like them too. Diesels offered them cleaner cabs, better visibility, emancipation from soot and smoke and, best of all, freedom from the constant concern over the levels of water in the watch glass and in the big tank aft. To desert railroaders this was no mean advantage for the local supplies of water were scanty and often contaminated with alkaline salts. To furnish the three million gallons of water per day that thirsty engines required to cross the arid wilderness and climb the steep grades of the Arizona Divide, the Santa Fe was obliged to operate large water treatment plants and run water trains the way some railroads ran company coal drags.

This is not to say that Diesels took all the challenge out of desert railroading. The heat, noise, vibration, and fumes that could be generated by a four-unit covered wagon climbing a steep grade under the hot southwestern sun were enough to tax the stamina of the hardiest of engine crews.

By the time 1943 arrived, the Santa Fe was moving aggressively to purchase enough FTs to Dieselize its through train movements across the deserts. Even when the War Production Board ordered EMD to concentrate its main efforts on the manufacturing of marine Diesel powerplants for the Navy, stopping production of passenger units entirely and slowing the building of freight units down to a mere trickle, the road managed to wrangle seventeen new A-B-B-A combination locomotives, which brought the Company's total Diesel fleet to 247 units operating as 139 engines.

Although the Diesels were making a strong bid to challenge the dominion of steam, the internal expansion engine, with 1,500 representatives, was still king on the Santa Fe lines. The War Production Board, partial to them on account of their more moderate demand for precision parts and scarce alloy steels, decreed that the Santa Fe would have to accept additional Texas and Northern types in lieu of the FTs which the road would have preferred. Therefore, new steam power was added to the roster throughout 1944. Meanwhile, the original batches of FTs continued to traverse the deserts running up colossal milage totals and generally proving themselves to be as valuable to the war effort as any of the more overt weapons that rode behind them.

With his side trip to Albuquerque completed, Delano returned to Belen to catch another freight heading west on March 24, 1943. This view was taken from the rear platform of the caboose as it clattered over the switch points near the yard's westernmost limits. A following section, powered by a 2-10-2 and a Baldwin Diesel switcher are drawn up on the adjacent ready tracks.

At Dalies, where the Belen Cutoff rejoins the original Santa Fe main line, the Conductor collects "19" orders handed up on a butterfly hoop by a woman operator. From here on, over the blistering New Mexico and Arizona deserts, we will be traveling on high density double tracked iron all the way to San Bernardino.

A 3750 class 4-8-4 rarely required a helper for any train during peacetime but wartime overloads dictated that even these long legged and powerful Northerns accept some help. It is hard to believe though, that a high wheeled Atlantic well past the prime of life could actually make much of a contribution to the progress of a first-class varnish haul. No. 1483 is one of a large tribe of 4-4-2 passenger engines built for the Santa Fe in 1910. Nicknamed "Bull Mooses" by the operating department, they sported 79″ drivers, superheaters, and balanced compounding and were the last word in the evolution of the Atlantic type locomotive intended for express passenger service. No. 3761, on the other hand, is an early series 4-8-4 built in 1928. The Santa Fe subsequently purchased two additional batches of Northerns built on essentially the same pattern but the earliest group, numbers 3751-3764 could always be distinguished from the others by the Elesco feedwater heater. This photo was taken trackside near Acomita, New Mexico.

This picture of a short work train fighting its way uphill through Acomita gives us an opportunity to survey the rocky, desolate chapparal of western New Mexico. Bridge traffic predominates overwhelmingly on this route for country like this generates very little on line revenue.

At Grants, New Mexico, a troop train is stopped on the eastbound main while its engine takes on water. Although troop trains were a common sight by early 1943, the specialized troop sleepers and kitchen cars were still rare and this train is obviously making do with nothing more elaborate — or comfortable — than ordinary tourist pull-mans. One hopes the men don't have too far to go in this outfit!

Delano's freight has gone into the hole at Thoreau to allow a Diesel streamliner powered by E-3 No. 12 to run around it. This pioneer motor and her sisters had a long life in the Santa Fe's service. After many years on transcontinental passenger runs and even more time spent in medium distance assignments, they were returned to EMD at La Grange for rebuilding. Emerging re-engined, re-contoured, and renumbered, they continued in service for another decade. An official Santa Fe publicity shot shows how No. 12's sister unit No. 2 looked when she emerged from the rebuilding process as No. 80. She retired in 1970 after 32 years in service.

Thoreau, incidentally, is where the Santa Fe crosses the Continental Divide at an elevation of approximately 7,000 feet.

In order to meet his need for a caster chair, this Santa Fe conductor improvised one out of a conventional piece of caboose furniture by the addition of electrical insulators giving each leg a smooth ball to skid over the rough planked floor of the buggy on.

Among his other duties, a brakeman was expected to master the fine art of cooking. In fact, his proficiency at this vital domestic chore often determined whether or not he got off the extra board and into a comfortable regular run, for conductors were known to pull strings and rank with great vigor and effectiveness when a pin puller with a reputation for culinary competence was up for grabs. During the war, caboose cookery became even more vital than usual for many crews were on continuous call, working sixteen hours out of every twenty-four, for days at a stretch. The crew of this train has not been home for three days and the brakeman's skill is their only guarantee of eating decently. Obviously, he has things well in hand.

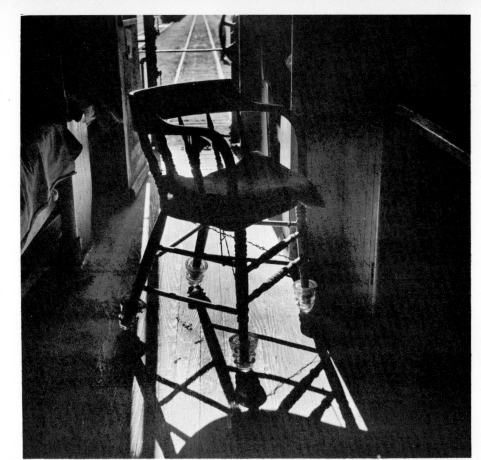

Delano made this shot just at dusk as his train waited to enter the yards at Gallup. The locomotive is from a following section that has run a few minutes behind all the way from Acomita. Now, with the day's run almost concluded, the trains bunch up while room is made for them to pull into the receiving tracks.

Near the crest of a small sag in Eastern Arizona, two cabooses whip past each other at speed. The usual hand signals attest that nothing is visibly amiss. *(Jack Delano Collection)*

This panorama shows some of the considerable activity to be seen at the east end of the yards at Winslow, Arizona. This subdivision headquarters is not only an important crew change point but also served as the main center of Diesel operations with shops, heavy repair facilities, and the largest pool of internal combustion freight units on the entire Santa Fe system. In early 1943, despite two years of concentrating Diesel power on the desert lines, it was still possible to see many more steam engines than F T units at Winslow, especially on the eastbound ready tracks. The Diesels, of course, worked westward, hoisting trains over the brutal grades to Kingman and Needles.

Typical of the yard goats assigned to the Arizona lines was No. 813, originally a Vauclain Compound Consolidation rebuilt into an 0-8-0 switcher. Oddly enough, she appears to be a coal burner, probably the last one that Delano encountered as he drew closer to the oil fields of Southern California. Two of the laborers in the foreground are members of the Navajo Tribe which was the Santa Fe's favorite source of track workers.

Made up into a four-unit "locomotive" totalling 4,500 horsepower, Motor No. 115 trundles down the yard to pick up her train. Notice that only the cab unit has road numbers prominently displayed on the front and sides of her exterior shell. The three booster units, not designed for independent operation, have very small numbers not readily visible so that they can be used with any cab without creating confusion as to the correct road number of the locomotive. Originally the FT units were intended to run as A-B-B-A combinations but due to wartime shortages of motive power the rear cab unit was often removed and combined with additional B units to make another locomotive. When that happened, a new number plate was installed over the coupler and the side numbers were adjusted to conform with the plate. After the war the FT locomotives were generally reconstituted as A-B-B-A combinations but between 1942 and 1945 it was common to see them running as A-B-B-B or A-B-B lashups.

The roundhouse at Winslow was in a transitional phase in 1943. Two years earlier it had been almost exclusively devoted to the care and servicing of a large fleet of 2-10-2s working over the mountains of Western Arizona. With the decision to concentrate Diesel freight power on the most arid and desolate portion of the desert, many of the ten-coupled hogs departed for new homes in California and F T "covered wagons" took over their vacated stalls. Still wedded to the basic mentality of steam operation, the Santa Fe's operating department attempted to stable the Diesels in these conventional facilities with indifferent success. Although the roundhouse arrangement is logical enough for steamers, it is definitely not the most convenient way to house multi-unit Diesel locomotives. In order to fit the stalls, the A-B-B-A combinations had to be broken in half and stored separately. When called for a run, the hostlers were obliged to get them onto the turntable in two sections and reassemble them on the roundhouse lead before turning them over to the road crews. When, as occasionally happened, the second pair of units lacked a cab, this arrangement became particularly awkward. Since fully hooded Diesels can generally be stored out of doors anyway, the roundhouse was soon replaced by servicing facilities more geared to the needs of internal combustion.

Standing in the cab of F T unit No. 109 as it pulls out of Winslow with a long freight on the drawbar, our eye falls naturally on the Copy 31 order on the engineer's clipboard. On this day, March 26, 1943, Second No. 7, the *Fast Mail and Express* operating daily between Chicago and Los Angeles is no less than five hours late, Winslow to Seligman. In wartime, under the stress of traffic that saw westbound freight tonnage increasing fivefold over peacetime totals in 1943 and tenfold by 1945, delays were inevitable despite the best intentions of the railroad. One archtypical story has a patron at some rural Kansas depot noting with approval the arrival of the *Scout* right on the advertised. Upon congratulating the station agent about this increasingly rare phenomenon he was informed "that's yesterday's *Scout*. She's exactly twenty-four hours late!"

Delano rode from Winslow to Kingman in the cab of No. 109, a stint that exposed him to the very essence of modern Diesel operations. Within two more years through freight traffic on this sector would be completely Dieselized, along with most of the major passenger runs, an

event that spared the Santa Fe the necessity of distributing hundreds of carloads of water to various points along the line for locomotive use. In 1943 the steam locomotive was still much in evidence hereabouts as witness this encounter with 4-8-2 No. 3736 heading east with a troop train in tow near Dennison. The husky Mountain was built by Baldwin in 1921.

This view was taken from the fireman's side of the cab as No. 109 rocked through the yards at Flagstaff. Engine crews trained on steam experienced difficulty in adjusting to the speeds at which Diesels took curves. The F T units generally had a much lower center of gravity than steamers plus considerably improved suspension systems and lateral springing. Their design reduced side sway and made for much better tracking on curves obviating the need to constantly slow down for them. This in turn led to a speeding up of freight train schedules and increased the capacity of a line that was almost saturated with traffic.

208

Looking over the engineer's shoulder, we get some idea of the sensation created by hurtling down on the town of Williams at 70 mph with nothing under us but two thin ribbons of steel. If the air brake lever and Johnson bar look familiar to those associated with steam engines, it is no accident. General Motors went out of its way to make Diesel controls similar to those of steamers in both appearance and function, thus, engineers making the switch from steam to Diesel operation could do so with a minimum of training and orientation. Normally, it took less than four student trips to qualify an experienced runner on Diesels and the changeover for firemen was even more pleasant!

We are near the town of Riordan at the crest of the Arizona Divide, 7,335 feet above sea level, the highest point on the Santa Fe west of Glorieta Pass in the Rockies. Our straining diesels have just accomplished a 96-mile climb with a ruling grade of 1.49% that started when we boarded at Winslow, where the elevation is approximately 4,843 feet. From here we drop down a steep grade to Ash Fork before tackling another eighteen miles of 1.42% ascending gradient to Crookton. Crookton was the last major summit westbound trains had to surmount before commencing a 149-mile drop to Needles which stands on the banks of the Colorado River at a mere 476 feet above sea level. This segment of the western slope of the Arizona Divide is actually the longest sustained mainline grade in the nation, a back-breaking, engine-straining climb with a ruling grade of 1.42%. During steam days, Ash Fork required 300 carloads of water delivered daily to quench the thirst of the hardworking 2-10-2s that dominated through traffic on this part of the line. In 1943, a four-unit Diesel was rated at 3,500 tons eastbound or 1,500 tons more than a 3800 Class Santa Fe Type. This was no mean advantage on a line that forwarded so many trains per day that no more could be accepted without throwing schedules off and inviting complete paralysis.

A string of typical Santa Fe water cars with a side door caboose cut into the middle waits on a yard lead at Ash Fork for the return to the water treatment plant on the banks of the Colorado River at Needles. Water cars could be distinguished from the more commonplace oil cars by their squatter, smaller expansion domes and by the legend stenciled on the car at the far right which reads "Engine water—do not unload at saltmarsh or pond".

Motor No. 109 is stopped on the main line while her brake shoes and wheels cool off some after a long drop down the 1.42% grade between Crookton and Seligman. Like No. 115, the 109 is an A-B-B-B combination which is less flexible than the usual A-B-B-A lash-up but served to keep booster units in service when cabs were in the shop. The number of F T units purchased by the Santa Fe eventually totalled 320.

Seligman, Arizona, was a major servicing point for westbound Diesels climbing the 96 miles of 1.5% ruling grade between Winslow and Riordan. While No. 109 was stopped here, Delano made this photograph of a woman teletypist and station agent. The Santa Fe hired its first woman employee back in 1874 when Mrs. Caroline Anderson became a clerk at the Topeka station. By 1929 approximately 1,000 women were on the payroll, nearly all of them office workers. In 1943, the number more than tripled and 3,500 women were on the job as signal tower operators, agents, freight handlers, turntable operators, yard clerks, track sweepers, shop helpers, engine wipers, timekeepers, storekeepers, and in several other capacities not usually open to them. These women workers were much different from the office "girls" of the peacetime years, being generally older and married, often with grown children in the Armed Forces.

Some idea of the desolate terrain and the drab, parched towns the Santa Fe passes through on its western Arizona lines can be gained from this picture of the tiny Mission style depot at Kingman. Indeed, only its importance as a helper terminal and train order relay insures that this town will continue to exist instead of joining the many ghost towns that dot the landscape in these parts.

At Kingman a double-headed freight extra holds the main while the engineers prepare their hogs for the steepest part of the grade leading up to the Arizona Divide. The ritual of oiling around the engine was a serious business during steam days, especially in the desert where blowing sand and grit were a major problem. To engine crews the operation was known as "greasing the pig".

For some reason the Santa Fe chose to abandon its traditional Mission
style architecture and build its Needles station in the form of a modified
Greek Revival edifice. Perhaps this layout provided more shade and
relief from the scorching rays of the desert sun.

California

The Santa Fe makes its entry into Southern California at the town of Needles, a hot dusty rail center situated on the bank of the Colorado River. Far from signifying the end of desert operations, Needles is the beginning of the deadly Mojave Basin, 200 miles of arid chapparal ending only at the crest of the San Bernardino and San Gabriel Mountains. Not until it has crossed this inferno and climbed the tortuous grades of Cajon Pass does the Santa Fe gain the verdant coastal lowlands that give substance to the legend of the Golden State.

Nor were physical difficulties the only problems that had to be overcome in order to secure access to the fabled coast. In the 1880s Santa Fe iron, under the banner of the Atlantic and Pacific Railroad, reached no further west then Needles where interchange with the Mojave Division of the Southern Pacific took place. The SP was, at that time, virtually the corporate monarch of California and blunted The Santa Fe's plans to penetrate this lush market by refusing to turn over any significant amount of traffic in spite of solemn agreements to share out the available business between its own line to El Paso and the A & P route. Faced with such obvious intransigence, the Santa Fe resolved to invade Southern California on the strength of its own right of way, a plan that called for considerable resources of capital and guile.

The first step in this process was the creation of the California and Southern Railway, secretly financed by the Santa Fe, to build a line from San Diego to Barstow. Work on this route began at San Diego in 1882 and had progressed as far northward as Colton before the directors of the Southern Pacific found out who the real backers of the C&S were. At Colton, it was necessary to effect a crossing of the Southern Pacific's main line over Beaumont Hill. Leaving no stone unturned, the SP corrupted local judges and sheriffs, raised armed posses, and instituted an outrageous series of delaying tactics to prevent the installation of the crossing. It seemed for a time as if the Santa Fe was headed for a confrontation as dramatic and dangerous as the one that had secured its right to build over Raton Pass but the Southern Pacific finally caved in under a Federal Court order. By the end of 1883 the tracks reached Barstow via Cajon Pass. The SP sold its now redundant Mojave Division to the A&P and all that remained for the Santa Fe to do was to build a line from San Bernardino to Los Angeles which became, to the surprise of many corporation strategists, the road's principal Pacific terminus.

The new properties proved to be a very profitable investment and by 1943 the line was double-tracked as far as Riverside and carried not only the Santa Fe's traffic but that of the Union Pacific as well. Building south from Salt Lake City, the UP had attained Dagett, just east of Barstow, in 1905. From here, its trains reached San Bernardino on the Santa Fe iron thanks to a trackage rights agreement quickly consummated between the two transcontinental giants.

Joint operation of the Cajon Pass line added immensely to the interest and excitement generated by this spectacular setting. There was dense traffic of every description, plenty of heavy grades and helper action. The colorful operating procedures included some of the last of the oldtime swing brakemen decorating car tops and setting up retainers by hand for the steep descending gradients in both directions. All this, carried out against the matchless backdrop of the mountains, made Cajon a mecca for all who would record the drama of railroading in the epoch of steam.

And beyond the hill was the sprawling complex of shops, yards, and facilities located at San Bernardino, the operational hub of Santa Fe's western lines which radiated north, south, and west throughout Southern and Central California. From here to our final destination at Los Angeles Union Station is the work of but a few more hours, a short level ride through the orange groves far removed from the somber midwinters of the East and the bleak deserts of New Mexico and Arizona.

Loading sand is not nearly as picturesque a part of preparing a steam locomotive for the road as taking on fuel and water. Nonetheless, naked steel drivers, even those bearing down on the rail surfaces with almost 150 tons of weight, often need a quick shot of grit to keep their footing when lugging heavy drags up the steep grades on either side of the Colorado River valley. Not just any sand will do, either. Pouring into the double domes of this massive 2-10-2 at Needles is grit of the highest quality, fine, dry, and loose to facilitate its flow through the pipes that will feed it to the skittish and slippery drivers at just the right moment.

War can complicate even a roundhouse wiper's job! Here a blackout hood has been swung aside to provide access to the headlight lens so that the traditional polishing that precedes every trip over the road can be expedited. Blackout regulations, inspired by a natural if groundless fear of Japanese air raids, specified that all locomotives operating within 250 miles of the Pacific Coast must carry hoods on all lights to prevent observation from the air. History does not record whether or not the innovation was successful in rendering locomotives significantly less visible but the fact that small hoods have even been fitted to the markers, at best mere pinpoints of white and green, testifies to the rigor of the law in this regard. Nor were the rear end markers neglected. Before departing Ludlow, this freight skipper is hanging up lights shaded in three directions.

With his markers properly hung, the conductor peers around the corner of his buggy's rear platform while the brakeman gives the highball. Two locomotives double-headed in the background belong to the inevitable following section which will trail the photographer's train as far as Barstow.

Nighttime on the Mojave Desert was often the most comfortable part of the operating day but in the middle of winter temperatures on the "Upper Desert", as this part of the Mojave is called, could plunge well below freezing. Here, three sections of a freight train wait to depart Barstow heading west. Markers glowing brightly in the clear, frigid air link the four locomotives together and proclaim that they shall follow each other at five-minute intervals and run one signal block apart at least as far as San Bernardino.

By day, the freight yards at Barstow give an impression of paralyzing congestion. Every siding is full almost to capacity with loads and empties. There is ample reason for this state of affairs because, in addition to being a major crew-changing and engine-servicing point, Barstow is where cars arriving from the East and destined for Northern California are separated from the main flow of Los Angeles - San Diego traffic and routed over the Tehachapi Loop to Bakersfield and San Francisco.

Another Union Pacific train is encountered west of Victorville double shotted for the heavy grade to Cajon Summit. The helper, 2-8-2 No. 2264 is a veteran of the First World War, having rolled out of the Baldwin Works in 1917 to join one of the largest fleets of Mikados ever owned by any railroad. Eventually, these sturdy and totally unglamorous workhorses found their way to every corner of the U.P. system from the Camas Prairie Line in Idaho to the Los Angeles Basin. The secret of their versatility lay in a judicious balance of qualities, a fair turn of speed, a useful amount of drawbar horsepower, and a moderate axleloading that allowed them to wander just about anywhere and perform a wide variety of jobs with distinction.

Traveling west out of Barstow, one cannot cover much ground without encountering the massively proportioned power of the Union Pacific Railroad. Its trains run between Daggett and San Bernardino on Santa Fe iron by virtue of a trackage rights agreement dating back to 1905 when the U.P.'s Los Angeles and Salt Lake Line was completed. No. 5098, here shown waiting on a siding at Victorville, is a splendid example of the distinctive locomotives produced by the U.P. in the mid-1920s when three-cylindered configurations were enjoying a brief vogue. The 5098 and her nine sisters are actually pioneers of the 4-10-2 wheel arrangement, a pattern copied by a few other systems, one being the Southern Pacific whose almost identical hogs followed these examples into service by about a year, arrogating to themselves the name of the class which remained the Southern Pacific type until the end of steam.

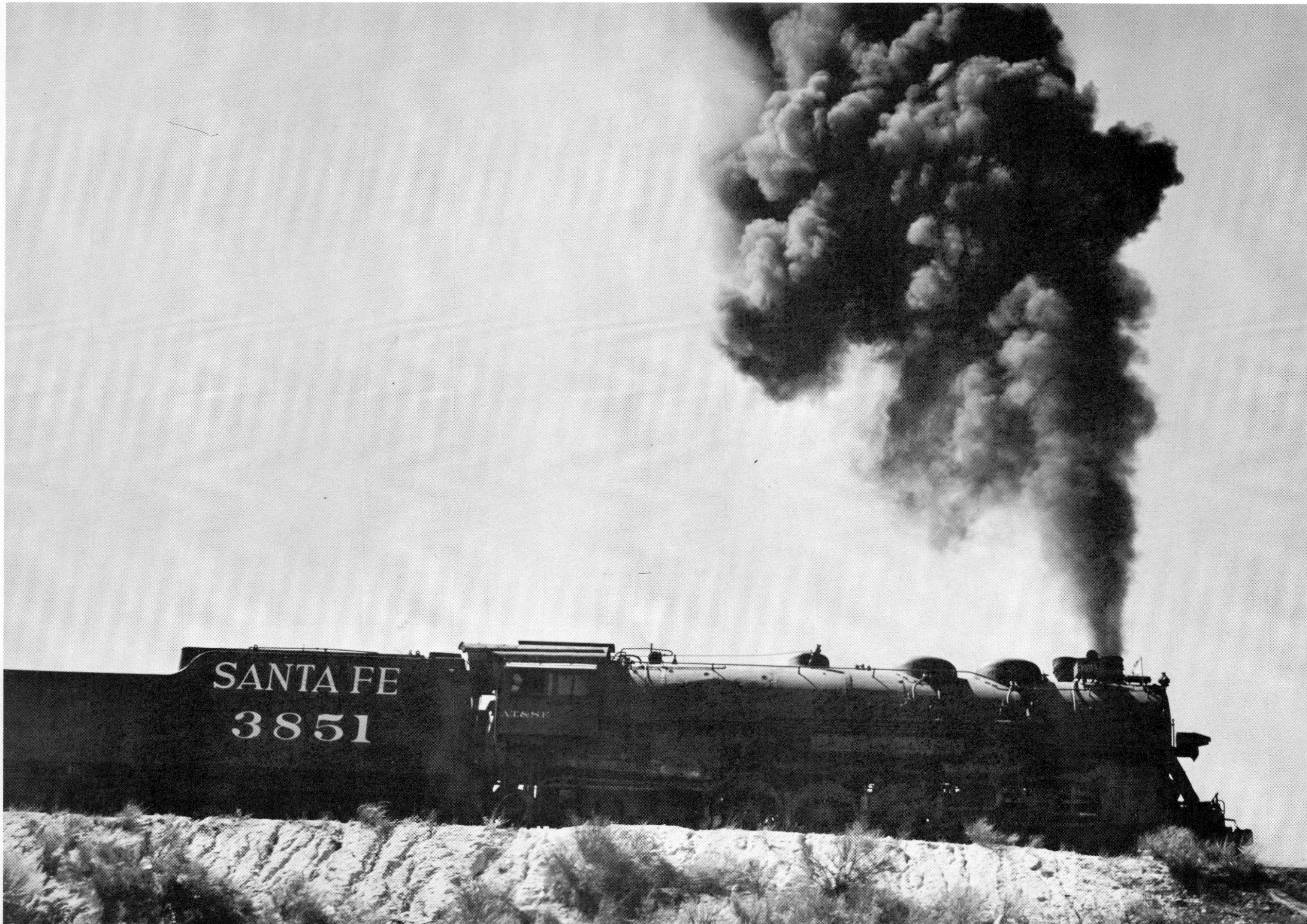
SANTA FE
3851

Freight trains on a heavy grade are often obliged to slog along at a pace not much above that of a plodding dray horse. On the eastern slope of the Cajon grade two of the Santa Fe's namesake 2-10-2s, reverse levers notched far forward to deliver the maximum amount of steam to the cylinders for each stroke, push and pull a lengthy drag of high cars towards the Summit. On this long and demanding grade there will be no adding or dropping the helper on the fly so the 3856 is sedately cut in ahead of the caboose to preserve its fabric from wracking stresses and to keep the markers in the rear where they rightfully belong. The 3800 class (Nos. 3800 - 3940) were the main freight power on the Santa Fe's Southern California lines. Delivered between 1919 and 1927, they represent the final development of the Santa Fe type.

224

Throughout the winter of 1943 rail replacement was going forward on the eastern approaches to Cajon Pass. This photo depicts a gang of Navajo Indians humping a new length of 131-lb. rail into position. Labor for track crews was in such short supply that by the end of 1944 the Santa Fe had even resorted to recruiting gandy dancers from among the interned Japanese at Owens Valley. To the surprise of the Company's officials, the Japanese workers proved to be the most trustworthy and productive of all the various tribes and nationalities that shouldered the task of helping to keep the tracks in order during those critical times. The end of the war saw the almost complete automation of all section hand work which brought an end to scenes like this.

Climbing the San Bernardino Mountains the trains pass through a rugged and desolate landscape of compelling drama and beauty. At this point, some ten miles southwest of Victorville, the grade is a stiff 2.2% and the summit has almost been attained. The immaculate condition of No. 3925 seems to indicate that she is recently out of the shops. Even her white flags have been laundered.

225

At Summit itself, the tracks diverge into three and then four sets, with a busy telegrapher's shack and a wye to facilitate helper turnaround. Lots of activity takes place here under the shadow of 10,064-foot Mt. San Antonio, locally known as "Old Baldy". The slow drags that have laboriously gained this goal often go into the hole to allow faster trains to run around them and to give their crews time to set up retainers for the steep drop into San Bernardino twenty miles farther south and 4,000 feet closer to sea level. Manning the car tops for this purpose are the train's three swing brakemen, each one responsible for some ten or fifteen cars.

226

Intent as they are on the task before them, these men can hardly spare a glance for the eastbound *Chief* which has just completed its own climb out of the San Gabriel Valley behind No. 3770, a Northern with 80″ drivers delivered new in 1938. This locomotive will run straight through to La Junta, Colorado, undergo a rapid servicing there and quickly depart with a westbound varnish run.

Within a mere 48 hours from this day, March 29, 1943,
No. 3770 will be seen again under the signal bridge just
beyond the northern limits of the San Bernardino Yard.
The endurance and fast turnaround of these 3750 class
Northerns was the wonder of the railroad industry and
exemplified the high state of the art of running steam
locomotives that the Santa Fe had attained.

Meanwhile our drag, having
received a highball indicating
that the swing brakemen
have finished their work,
rocks past the order board
and begins its descent amid
a haze of smoke acrid with
the smell of hot metal.

Badly burned by its own experiments with articulated power back in the drag freight era, the Santa Fe disdained the use of Mallets on the Cajon line and relied on its 3800 class 2-10-2s to shoulder the burden of both road and helper assignments. The Union Pacific was more adventurous with regard to motive power and consequently we are gratified with the sight of a brand new Challenger, No. 3931, Alco class of 1942, waiting in a siding just south of Summit for another train to run around it. Scenes such as this were common on Cajon Pass because the line through here is not an orthodox double track operation. Instead, it consists of two single track mains built at different times and each carrying independently routed traffic in both directions.

At the western approach to Cajon Pass the rear end helper of an easbound freight is cut off to take water at a plug conveniently located at the foot of the grade. A flagman protects against following traffic while the engine crew trims their fire and blows down the boiler to clear the mud rings preparatory to tackling the grade in earnest.

After so many days in Santa Fe cabooses, it's almost refreshing to view an example from another road. The Union Pacific buggy pictured here represents the latest practice on that system with the cupola centered and built up somewhat higher than was usual on earlier models.

At the north end of the San Bernardino Yards stands the handsome passenger station which houses the main administrative offices for this district. Steam and Diesel switch engines bustle about their business with a commendable lack of smoke. Perhaps those dark rows of windows in the station have something to do with that. There's no telling what brass hat may be lurking behind them checking to see which crews are reading the smoke abatement notices posted with monotonous regularity wherever engine crews congregate.

A lone 3800 class helper drifting down the 1.5 percent western approach grade makes a small impression when beheld against the mighty ramparts of Old Baldy. It's easy to see why the Santa Fe crews refer to this singular hunk of almost perpendicular real estate simply as "the Mountain".

In this picture, a busy yard goat takes time out to pose briefly for the camera. The switchman riding the foot-board seems so assured that one can only conclude that the "Keep Off" warnings stenciled on the pilot beam are not meant for him. Note the blackout hoods fitted to the switch lamps, mute reminders that there's a war on in a scene otherwise prosaic in its normality.

Working our way south through the yards, we run across an early Alco Diesel switcher. Although No. 2326 is obscure in rank and station, she is more than just a pawn in the railroad game for it was switching service that first brought the Diesel electric locomotive to the railroads. Faced with a growing clamor for smoke abatement in the conjested terminals of the East Coast, management turned to the Diesel almost in desperation. Once in service, the original Diesel yard goats not only solved the smoke problem but exhibited other virtues as well. Still, it was almost ten years before a reliable Diesel electric road engine was produced. By 1943, Diesel switchers were a well established part of the railroad scene, much more so than their more publicized cousins on the road where it could still be plausibly argued that new developments in steam technology, improved rotary cam valves, Geisel steam ejectors, turbines, or something even more exotic, might yet halt the Diesel tide and save the day for the traditional Iron Horse. None cared to challenge the supremacy of the Diesel in yard service, however. No. 2326 and her sisters were here to stay!

Some idea of the scope and complexity of operations originating in the San Bernardino yards can be gained from a glance at the call board situated in the crew's locker room. The 1st District board, upon which the caller is now chalking up his assignments, covers the line from San Bernardino to Los Angeles via Pasadena. The "Helper" slots on the left-hand board do not refer to engine crews but to swing brakemen who rode all freight trains over the Summit to help set up retainers on the downhill portions.

Overshadowing everything else in the San Bernardino yards are the sprawling shops which, in 1943, had the responsibility of maintaining and repairing all Santa Fe steam power west of the Rockies. As such, they were a critical link in the strategic role played by the Santa Fe in the Pacific Theater of War and a principal industry of the town of San Bernardino. Here, they can be seen looming over a pair of Union Pacific helpers about to do battle with the Cajon Grade. The U.P. hogs are a grimy pair and none too modern, for the road kept its most up-to-date power at work on its principal main line 500 miles farther north.

A general view of the main erecting hall of the shops shows them working to capacity on a large assortment of engines both new and old. Note how much longer the boiler of Northern No. 3766 is than those of the Pacific and Mountain Types in this picture. It was here in the San Bernardino shops that the first practical oil burning locomotive was developed 'way back in 1894 when the Southern California Railway's No. 10 was put into freight service on an experimental basis working over Cajon Pass.

Inside the shops, the feminine touch is everywhere. Although some women actually worked as mechanics helpers, performing heavy repairs requiring at least some training, the majority of shop women functioned primarily as sweepers, wipers, or in other custodial capacities. One customary task was the routine cleaning of locomotive parts and components, traditionally a helper's task, that required no great amount of training or strength but was a vital first step in setting the stage for more complex mechanical activities. Roller bearings about to be fitted into journals must be meticulously cleaned of protective grease before being checked for trueness while the driving axles of a massive 4-8-4 also require considerable devoted labor to free them from the thick accumulation of road grime picked up in months of hard service. The two ladies in leather aprons will see to these tasks and many others, thus freeing the male helpers to concentrate on the more arduous and demanding jobs that abound in the shops.

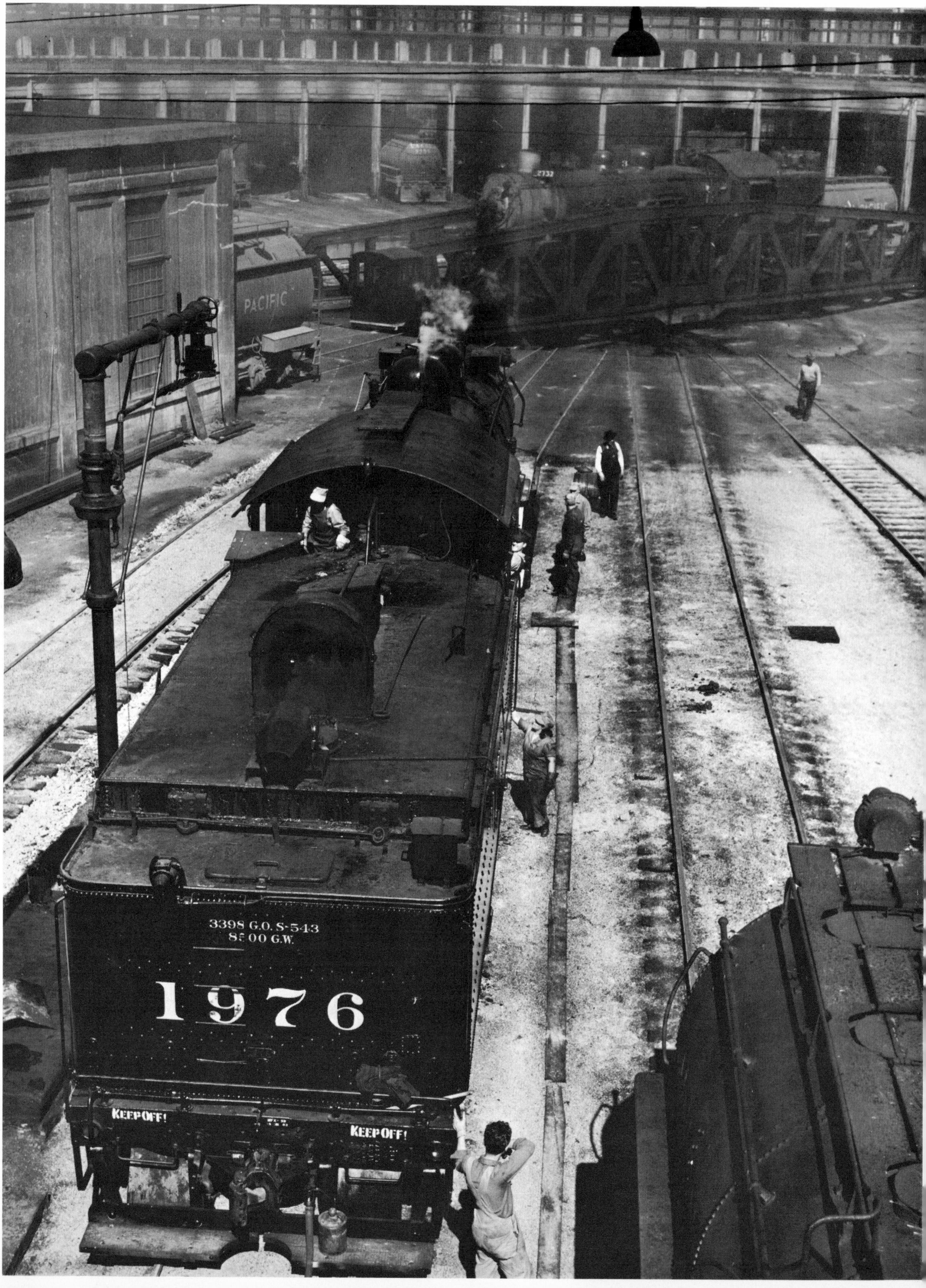
PACIFIC
3398 G.O. S-543
8500 G.W.
1976
KEEP OFF!
KEEP OFF!

A closer look, focusing more directly on Consolidation No. 1976 reveals yet another change, notably the presence of two women recently installed as replacements for male workers promoted to traincrewmen or lost to the Armed Forces. While the hostler spots the little hog under the fuel spigot, our two robust representatives of the fair sex will fill and trim her lamps and see that her various lubricators are topped off with valve oil, crosshead grease, and other essentials to smooth operation. Small, elderly engines like the 1976 were usually employed by the Santa Fe on the various routes between San Bernardino and Los Angeles where grades are light and there is a good deal of slow local traffic unworthy of the talents of larger, more modern engines.

The final step in returning a freshly shopped locomotive to the road is to break it in under light load conditions taking care to handle the controls with some delicacy until it can be established that valves and packing glands are seating properly, bearings are running cool, pipe joints are tight and well sealed, and there are no forgotten wads of cotton waste obstructing lubricating lines or other vital passages. In some instances this meant a few days' duty hauling short distance locals or, as in the case of this massive Santa Fe type, a brisk session on the slip track, a carefully greased section of rail back of the shops where the engine can be run for hours on end at a variety of speeds. This will assure that the shopmen's handiwork will not be subjected to the scrutiny of the operating department until satisfaction can be guaranteed.

(Overleaf) During more normal times the Union Pacific used its own engine servicing facilities to stable power working the Cajon Pass run. The wartime emergency had, however, forced the U.P. and the Santa Fe into even closer collaboration than was their accustomed habit and the Santa Fe's "San Berdoo" Roundhouse is seen here playing host to a trio of veteran U.P. Mikes. The visitors, with their Sweeney stacks, Vanderbilt tenders, and other less tangible Harriman features are very conspicuous indeed as they ride the turntable or sit interspersed among the square tanked natives.

It was not until very late in the war that a few women began to land jobs as engineers on electrified commuter trains in the east or as firemen on a few western lines where oil fuel was used. It is obvious from the photo below, however, that by 1943 they were entrusted with the operation of other mechanical contrivances in the domain of the Iron Horse. In fact, at the San Berdoo Roundhouse they seem to have taken over the turntable quite completely, once again freeing male personnel for some other field of endeavour. Indeed, the women often surprised the Santa Fe's management with their efficiency and quickly acquired skills. In prewar days, a roundhouse would have been one of the first places on any railroader's list of worksites that were "no place for a woman." In actuality, some roundhouse jobs were not particularly taxing and any girl who was not unduly put off by loud noises, smoke, greasy tracks, and dark gloomy engine stalls could fit in with little trouble.

Before departing San Bernardino for the last leg of the journey to Los Angeles there is just time to make a brief excursion to the northern yard limits to witness the return of No. 3770 last seen heading east two days earlier at the summit of Cajon Pass.

A time exposure of the Los Angeles Yards by night reveals one of the glaring (no pun intended!) inconsistencies of the wartime blackout regulations. The inconspicuousness of the carefully hooded switch lanterns is totally destroyed by the brightly lit street overpass! The ragged line of white light visible in this picture is the path of a lantern-toting switchman out of the yard office, across several tracks to the footboards of a switch engine, and thence for a short ride into the background.

Far smaller and less elaborate then the yard complex at San Bernardino are the Santa Fe's freight terminal facilities at First Street just north of Redondo Junction near downtown Los Angeles. This yard, although modest in scope, was the final stop for transcontinental freight on the Santa Fe. From here, the cars will be made up into short cuts for delivery to east Los Angeles, Redondo Beach, or Wilmington by way of various feeder lines extending across the Los Angeles Basin.

Los Angeles Union Station was a busy place during the war. In these two Santa Fe Company photos, servicemen are shown debarking from their spartan tourist sleepers and enjoying a meal at the Harvey House. When large groups of G.I.s had to be accommodated, Fred Harvey's doors were closed to the public and zealously guarded by armed Military Policemen. Despite the pressures of war and a general indifference to the plight of the wartime traveler, Harvey House standards of quality and service remained largely intact. One can be sure that men in the picture are reasonably satisfied. Mess Hall food was never like this! (*Santa Fe Railway Company*)

From Redondo Junction, the Santa Fe dispatched many local freights to meander among the citrus groves and oil derricks picking up and setting out revenue cars of every variety and description. Mikado No. 3121 was typical of the power assigned to such runs, a humble toiler shuffling patiently back and forth between Los Angeles and San Bernardino with several of her sisters, all of them well past the prime of their lives. While awaiting clearance to depart for Pasadena and points east, her crew gathers around the white-haired trainmaster for the time-honored ritual of talking over their orders and comparing watches.

Jack Delano's Written Accounts

■ ■

JACK DELANO'S WRITTEN ACCOUNT
OF HIS TRIP FROM CHICAGO TO
CLINTON AND RETURN

Every day between 11:00 a.m. and 1:00 p.m. several high-speed freights leave Proviso Yard bound for the West Coast. The first division point west of Chicago is Clinton, Ia. This story concerns

one of these trains, No. 251, and its crew on one of its trips from Proviso to Clinton and return.

The crew reported about 11:30 to find the train in the classification yard still being made up. The rear brakeman went straight to the caboose where he attended to such things as hanging out the markers, checking the supply of torpedoes and fusees, and etc. The head brakeman had in the meantime reported to the roundhouse with the engineer and fireman to collect the locomotive and bring it to the train. The conductor was at the yard office getting his waybills, train orders, and clearance.

As soon as the train was made up the engine was coupled on and the brakemen began their inspection of the train. Starting at each end, they walked the length of the train on one side until they met in the middle. Next, they changed sides and walked back again, testing the air of each car, releasing handbrakes, watching for dragging brake rods and shoes and giving each car a general cursory inspection. Arriving back at the rear of the train the brakeman notified the engineer to test the brakes by signaling "apply" and "release". With everything normal the train was ready to depart.

The conductor came from the yard office bringing train orders for the engineer. Since running will be by automatic train control, the engineer handed the ATC key to the conductor who will keep it in the caboose until arrival at Clinton. (This procedure is followed to prevent the engineer from tampering under any circumstances with the train control mechanism). The highball sign was given and the powerful H class engine started the train smoothly out of the yard. The conductor caught the caboose as it pulled past the spot where he had been conferring with the head-end crew.

The crew consisted of five men: the conductor, John M. Wolfsmith, rear brakeman Clarence Averill, head brakeman William Strocheim, engineer John Johnson, and fireman William Morrison.

On this occasion their train, the first section of No. 251, engine No. 3014, carried 57 loads and eight empties: steel, 9 cars; government freight, 10 cars; machinery, 5 cars. The rest consisted of tables, pipe, tubing, charcoal, stone, lumber, furniture, auto parts, insecticide, bottles, paper, coke briquettes, bakery goods, malts, and other items. Almost the entire consist was bound straight for the West Coast via the Union Pacific.

The first stop was at De Kalb, Ill., for coal, water, and inspection. Since time was short, the brakemen walked only one side of the train, the downwind side, which would allow them to smell hotboxes on the opposite, hidden side. From De Kalb, first No. 251 made straight for Clinton reaching a maximum speed of 63 mph (the maximum that automatic train control would allow). In the caboose the conductor worked on his reports while the brakeman signaled passing trains and control towers and flagged a train that was coming up on them at a siding. Sandwiches were toasted on the caboose stove and the train arrived at Clinton at 4:35 p.m. The engine was uncoupled and taken to the roundhouse. The rear-end crew caught a ride to the yard office in the cab of the following section's engine, No. 3016, made their report, and went to a rooming house to spend the night.

They stayed at the house of Mrs. Disher. This was a private home that had been converted into a rooming house accommodating 14 men. It was run by Mrs. Disher and her daughter Lucille whose father had been an engineer for forty years before his death in 1930. The house catered exclusively to railroad workers, most of whom came regularly every other night. The rate was fifty cents per night and little envelopes were kept in a box in the vestibule to enable the men to pay for their lodging at times when everyone was asleep. A blackboard in the hallway listed the names of the men who were staying there that night and the rooms they occupied. This was both

for the convenience of the men who often seek out friends that way and also for the "caller" who came to notify the train crewmen of impending runs.

After washing up, the men had dinner either at the depot or at a lunchroom around the corner and then spent the evening playing cards, telling tall stories, bowling, or having a few beers. Most went to bed early in anticipation of being called before dawn the next day.

Sure enough, the caller woke them at 5:30 the next morning and after a light breakfast they reported to the yard office while the engineer and fireman went to the roundhouse to get engine No. 3016. The train they were to take back to Proviso was an extra and consisted of 57 loads, mostly perishables, and 7 empties. Train orders read in part as follows: "Operate carefully where fog exists . . .", "Restrict speed to 20 mph from mile post 65 to Malta Depot account damaged track" and "Look out for material along south side of westbound main track in front of depot at Dixon . . ." After several delays, including one due to a streamliner blocking the main line at the depot, Extra 3016 East departed Clinton at 9:00 a.m.

Only one stop was made at Nelson, Illinois, for coaling and inspection. The train was delivered into the receiving yard at Proviso at 2:00 p.m. The crew rode in the engine cab to a little railroad station where they could get a passenger train into town.

JACK DELANO'S WRITTEN ACCOUNT OF A DAY SPENT RIDING TRAINS ON THE INDIANA HARBOR BELT RAILROAD

This is the story of a train crew's work day on the Indiana Harbor Belt Railroad. This line is one of several in the Chicago area whose function it is to connect the various eastern and western systems that enter Chicago. The Indiana Harbor Belt forms a semicircle around the outskirts of Chicago from its northern terminus at Franklin Park to Indiana Harbor and nearby points in Indiana.

The five-man crew consisting of conductor Lawson W. Cunningham, engineer Joseph Stites, fireman Lawrence Adams, head brakeman Lee High, and rear brakeman Louis Zerkel, reported for work at 11:30 a.m. These men work out of a pool and are called at irregular hours as they are needed. The engineer and fireman checked in at the roundhouse where they were assigned an engine already coaled and watered and set off to pick up the caboose. The conductor and brakemen reported to the yardmaster's office where they received instructions for their trip.

On this particular delivery they were to go to Proviso Yard light to pick up a train to be taken to Blue Island. At Blue Island they would pick up yet another train, delivery instructions to come later.

They left Norpaul yard at Franklin Park at 12:10 p.m. and arrived at Proviso at 12:20. There, they picked up a train consisting of 45 loads and six empties. After routine inspection of this consist the conductor reported to the yard office where he was given his waybills and conferred by telephone with the IHB dispatcher before departing for Blue Island. The train carried a variety of cargo including machinery, canned goods, lumber, malt, scrap, milk, castings, and much more, all of it bound for interchange with eastern railroads.

Conductor Cunningham's train arrived at Blue Island at 3:15 p.m. The caboose was uncoupled and sent down a siding while the rest of the train headed straight for the icehouse because there were six reefers that needed re-icing. That was as far as their delivery was to go. From here on, the train would either be picked up directly by the New York Central and forwarded east or sent over the hump and broken down for incorporation into other trains.

While the engine crew went to the service tracks for coal and water the conductor reported to the yard office where he received instructions to pick up another train for delivery to the Erie Railroad at Hammond. After coupling up and making the necessary inspections they departed from Blue Island at 4:55 p.m.

This train was mainly composed of a large shipment of meat that was supposed to make connections with the Erie at 6:00 p.m. so that it could arrive at the market in New York by the next morning. However, they were considerably delayed when a derailment experienced by a preceding train at Calumet City forced them to make a long detour through the Chesapeake and Ohio and Wabash yards in order to reach Hammond. Final delivery was not made until 8:45 p.m.

As soon as they reached the Erie yard at Hammond, the train was blue flagged and a crew of car inspectors went to work. There being no load for the crew to take back, they left Hammond light to return to Norpaul Yard, making a twenty-minute lunch stop at Calumet City and a brief stop at Blue Island for water and orders. They left Blue Island at 10:50 p.m. and arrived at Norpaul at 11:45 making a total work day of almost twelve hours.

LETTER FROM JACK DELANO TO ROY STRYKER, HEAD OF THE OWI PHOTOGRAPHIC SECTION

Author's note: Those whose interest in trains and railroading have led them to a secondary preoccupation with cameras and photography will doubtless enjoy this account of Mr. Delano's tribulations in compiling his photodocumentary on railroad activity in and around Chicago.

January 13, 1943
Chicago, Ill.

Dear Roy:

I have just come back from the second of the two train trips I told you about on the phone. The first was on the Indiana Harbor Belt Railway on a trip they made from the North Western to the Erie Railroad. The second was a round trip on a North Western train from Chicago to Clinton, Iowa and return. I am sending you the film and captions for both stories.

For the first trip, I got out to the Belt railroad yard at ten in the morning, looked over the yard, took some shots of the crew checking in, and departed a little after twelve. There was just the engine and a caboose. We were going to Proviso yard to pick up a train there and deliver it to the Blue Island yard, pick up still another train there and deliver it to the Erie.

I tried to get as complete a story of the trip and the crew as possible, but there were several things I had to learn while I was working. One of the first is that I could not be in two places at the same time — that is, at the caboose end and at the engine end. The distance between the two might be anything from a quarter of a mile to over a mile and it was impossible to be running back and forth because stops were short and the train would start long before I got to either end. So I learned to hop on the caboose while the train was in motion. After many clumsy starts I got over the fear of being left behind and was able to get off when the train stopped for short intervals and take several shots. (I still need *both* my hands to hop on and let one of the brakemen get on with my camera).Once in the caboose I learned another lesson from bitter experience: don't stand up in a caboose unless you hold on to something, otherwise you and your camera may go flying through the rear of the train.

Other than taking a few shots of the engineer and fireman, there is not much point in riding in the engine cab. It is very difficult to see out of the cab and quarters are very crowded, so I spent most of my time in the caboose. When there is switching to do, however, the engine is the place to be and I was always having to work out a compromise on the basis of what I could expect at the next stop.

I could take along with me only a limited amount of equipment—just what I could carry in my arms and *on my back*. Railroad yards are usually far from train or bus stops and walking is the only means of transportation. Although I took the Graphic along I was seldom able to use it, and had to rely a great deal on the Rollie. Trying to stand in a caboose and take pictures is worse than in any rocking boat and I had to shoot all the pictures at very fast shutter speeds. Anyhow, there is not much room inside the caboose and the wider angle of the Rollie was a great help. As usual, the weather remains bad and shooting with the Graphic was very often impossible.

All this experience was very helpful when I took the trip to Clinton. I had hoped to come back from Clinton with a cattle train but thought it better to get a complete story on the same crew I came out with. Since they were taking back with them a manifest freight of vegetables and fruit the cattle story is being held for a little

later. The Chicago and North Western hauls two sorts of cattle trains out of Clinton, one bound for the stock yards in Chicago and the other a through train with cattle for the East Coast. I hope to be able to do both.

The difficulty all along during my work here (aside from the weather) has been the extensive arrangements and formalities, the unavoidable delays which take up so much time. When an appointment has been made and the great picture taking day has finally come, I am just as likely to encounter fog, snow, sleet, or an eclipse of the sun.

The long hours of sitting in the caboose has produced a wonderful crop of "bull shooters". Every time two railroad workers get together they take their trips all over again. Toward the end of my trip on the Belt line, we were heading back home and although the little coal stove in the caboose kept us cozy and comfortable it was bitter cold outside. The conversation naturally centered around the weather. The conductor told a story about such a night when they found a man who had been locked in a refrigerator car and had almost frozen to death.

The brakeman had a story too. It seems he was working on the lead one night in below zero weather. He was getting off a car when he noticed a figure lying beside one of the switches. He went over and saw a guy lying there frozen stiff. "He was frozen so solid we had to use a board to pry his hands apart. At first we thought he was dead but then we decided to take him into the caboose and warm him up. We laid him down on a bunk but none of us could stay there because we had to go back to work. We figured we'd come back in a little while and see how he was coming along. A little later we returned to the caboose thinking that we'd better call an ambulance and get the stiff to the hospital. We opened the door and there was our stiff sittin' up straight with blankets all around him and yelling "Shut that g-d door, there's a f---draft in here!"

Thanks for sending me the replacement camera so promptly. The damage to my old camera occurred while I was working at one of the yards. It was one of those days when the ground was covered with a sheet of ice that was hidden by a light snowfall. I was climbing off a car and found myself lying on the ground instead of standing. Fortunately for the camera I was still clutching it in my hand and had not let it drop. The bed was slightly bent, knocking the lens out of alignment. I hope it won't take too long to have it repaired.

Regards to Alice and Phyllis and everyone in the office.

Jack

JACK DELANO'S NOTES CONCERNING OPERATING CONDITIONS ON THE SANTA FE RAILWAY DURING HIS TRIP

Author's note: The following remarks have been culled from a much longer memorandum written by Mr. Delano on the subject of his OWI railroad assignment. Much of this information deals with the basics of railroading and has been deleted because it has already been covered in the picture captions. What remains to be included here are specific facts and details that give the reader some further insight into the Santa Fe's activities in 1943.

During this trip there was much evidence that the Santa Fe was handling the greatest volume of business in its history. Preference was given at all times to military cargo and personnel. We met troop trains on every part of the line — sometimes as many as ten in one day. A trainmaster at one of the yards in the Southwest told me that on several occasions they had handled as many as fifteen troop movements in a 24-hour period. In one instance we met a double header with 30 empty tourist coaches returning for another contingent after having discharged its original load of troops.

The further west we went, the greater seemed to be the congestion of traffic in the freight yards. According to the estimates of the various trainmasters they were forwarding 38 trains a day at Ft. Madison, 30 freights and 6 passenger trains at Wellington, 60 to 70 trains, including 22 passenger consists, through Needles. Corwith Yard in Chicago handled 1,012,000 cars in 1942 as compared with 692,000 in 1929 and 460,000 in 1933. At Argentine Yard, the largest on the system, 2,145,000 cars were handled in 1942, an increase

of 300,000 over the 1941 total. The agent at the Santa Fe freight depot in Kansas City told me they did $1,500,000 worth of business during the month of February, 1943 — an increase of 37% over the corresponding month in 1942.

Although train orders are the main method of controlling traffic on the Santa Fe, various types of automatic signal systems are used along the entire route. Between Pequot, Illinois, and the Mississippi River Bridge, a distance of 174 miles, trains are governed by automatic train control. For a distance of twelve miles west of Kansas City a track reversal system is used, allowing trains to be operated in both directions on either main line. Electrically controlled automatic switches shunt the trains from one track to another. The remainder of the route which I traveled is equipped with an automatic block signal system.

In many places, such as the single track districts in New Mexico and in the Needles - Barstow - San Bernardino section of California, traffic was particularly heavy. Freight trains sometimes waited hours to get into the yards. We had to wait three hours at Texico, New Mexico, because the yard at Clovis was full. The conductor said that they often had to wait longer. Between Needles and San Bernardino many sidings were filled with trains waiting because the yards were filled to capacity. Crews told of often having to be on duty for 16 hours (the maximum permitted by law) and still not completing their runs. Other crews had to be "deadheaded" out to bring the trains in. The run from Needles to Barstow, a distance of 167 miles, takes about eight or nine hours under normal conditions. The conductor of our train said he never made it in less than 16 hours now. We had left Needles at 10:45 a.m. but only got as far as Ludlow where one train was already on a siding waiting to get into Barstow. Leaving this crew with their drag, I took a passenger train into Barstow. Inquiring about them at midnight, I learned that they were still not in yet.

While congestion seemed to be greatest in Southern California, it was also serious in other places. The single track district between Clovis and Belen, New Mexico, for example, was having a particularly hard time. In addition to the traffic burden, this area is so dry that water must come

254

from wells over 2000 feet deep. Between Vaughan and Agudo there are no wells at all. A 200-mile pipeline owned by the Southern Pacific brings water to Vaughan where it is purchased by the Santa Fe and carried in tank cars to watering stations along the line. This water train makes a round trip each day.

Under the supervision of roadmasters, section gangs and road crews of the maintenance of way department make all necessary repairs or changes in the track and roadbed. Present manpower conditions have caused shortages of workers that are much more severe among the lower paid workers than they are in the skilled trades. Many section hands have gone into the armed services. Others readily leave their jobs for better pay elsewhere. Consequently, labor turnover is great. Forty-three Indian section hands were working when I arrived at Needles out of a crew of 150 the day before. The others had left because better pay was promised them at a nearby construction site.

There was a shortage of switchmen and brakemen at almost every yard but particularly in the West. At Barstow for example, men were often found working 16-hour tricks and some of them had been away from home for two or three days. Sleeping accommodations were hard to find and some of the men carried blanket rolls with them. Others slept in cabooses which were not very comfortable because they are stored on the caboose track and every time one is picked up or set out the whole line is jolted.

Getting food was another problem. While some of the men prepared meals in their cabooses, conductors and brakemen off the extra board were shifted around a great deal and had no regular caboose of their own to keep food in. Taking along a few sandwiches was hardly adequate for men going off for the whole day not knowing whether or not they would be able to get a hot meal after 16 or more hours on duty. At most of the sidings at which stops were made traincrews could rarely get more than fuel and water for the locomotive. Sometimes soldiers for an Army camp along the right of way would bring them sandwiches and coffee from their canteen.

To ease the labor shortage on the Western lines, men were being shifted from the East. San Bernardino Yard had just received a contingent of 10 switchmen from Ft. Madison. One of the brakemen on my Barstow to San Bernardino train had come from Kansas City and was soon to be promoted to a yardmaster and assigned to Barstow. Nineteen other switchmen were similarly on their way west from Argentine. Increasing use was also being made of women workers as freight handlers, car cleaners, locomotive shop sweepers, car inspectors, and roundhouse helpers. Women were likewise beginning to take over some of the clerical jobs traditionally held by men.

Index

▪ ▪

° Denotes picture reference

— A —

Abo, New Mexico, 169, 186°, 187
Abo Pass, 131, 169
Acomita, New Mexico, 197, 199, 202
Albuquerque, New Mexico, 189, 190, 191-193, 196
Albuquerque Division, AT&SF RR, 195
Albuquerque Shops, AT&SF RR, 192, 193°
Alton Limited, the, (passenger train), 39
Alton RR (Baltimore & Ohio subsidiary), 36°, 37, 39, 115
Amarillo, Texas, 152, 169, 170°, 171, 172°, 173
Anderson, Caroline, 212
Argentine Yard, AT&SF RR, 123, 142-147
Arizona Divide, the, 195, 211, 213
Ash Fork, Arizona, 211
Atlantic and Pacific RR, (AT&SF subsidiary), 215
Atchison, Topeka & Santa Fe Rwy., 5-6, 21, 25, 115, 122-249

— B —

Baker County, Oregon, 18
Baltimore & Ohio RR, 18, 21, 26, 39, 109, 143
Bangor & Aroostook RR, 18
Barstow, California, 195, 215, 218-221
Barstow Yard, AT&SF RR, 218, 219°, 220
Belen, New Mexico, 169, 178, 184, 187, 196
Belen Cutoff (Pecos Division) AT&SF RR, 169, 175, 184, 189, 197
Belen Yard, AT&SF RR, 187, 188°, 196
Belt Operating Agreement of 1912, 97
Bensonville, Illinois, 75, 112, 116-117
Belva, Oklahoma, 167
Benton, Thomas Hart, 161
Big Spring, Texas, 21, 23
Bingham Canyon, Utah, 33
Black, Texas, 173
Blue Island, Illinois, 75, 99, 103, 104, 106, 107
Buchanan, New Mexico, 182

— C —

Cajon Pass, 215-216, 221-231, 236
Calumet City, Illinois, 109, 110
Canyon, Texas, 173
Caribou, Maine, 18
Carson City, Nevada, 12
Chattanooga, Tennessee, 23, 25, 26
Chattanooga Yard, CNO&TP RR, 25
Chief, the, (passenger train), 25, 227
Chicago, Illinois, 5, 35, 37, 39, 43, 45, 47, 49, 56, 71, 75, 80, 91, 97, 116, 117, 118, 123, 175, 195
Chicago, Burlington & Quincy RR, 37, 39, 40°, 112, 115, 143
Chicago, Rock Island & Pacific RR, 79, 119, 143
Chicago Switching Limits, 97
Chicago, Minneapolis, St. Paul & Pacific RR, 112, 116-117
Chicago & North Western RR, 5, 45-77, 79-95
Chicago Terminal District, 47
Chicago Union Station, 35-44, 45
Chillicothe, Illinois, 123, 129-131
Cicero, Illinois, 2
City of Denver, the, (passenger train), 71, 72-73°, 78
City of Los Angeles, the (passenger train), 71, 72-73°

City of Portland, the (passenger train), 78
Cimarron River Valley, 167
Cincinnati, New Orleans & Texas Pacific RR, (Southern RR subsidiary), 25
Cleveland, Ohio, 115
Clewiston, Florida, 11
Clinton, Iowa, 53, 71, 77, 79, 80, 87, 88, 91
Clovis, New Mexico, 164, 169, 173, 175, 176
Clovis Roundhouse, AT&SF RR, 175-176
Colorado River, the, 211, 215, 217
Continental Divide, the, 175, 200
Corn King Limited, the, (passenger train), 45
Corwith Yard, AT&SF RR, 115, 122-128
Crookton, Arizona, 211, 212
Curtis, Oklahoma, 167, 168

— D —

Dalies, New Mexico, 189, 197
Delano, Jack, 5-6, 35, 37, 44, 45, 59, 91, 103, 107, 112, 118, 123, 128, 134, 139, 142, 143, 148, 182, 184, 187, 196, 200, 202
Dennison, New Mexico, 208
Denver Zephyr, the (passenger train), 41
Denver & Rio Grande Western RR, 13, 15, 17, 123
Dilworth, Richard, 39
Durango, Colorado, 13, 15, 17
Durango Roundhouse, D&RGW RR, 14°, 15

— E —

Eastern Division, AT&SF RR, 155
Ellinor, Kansas, 169
Emporia Junction, Kansas, 143, 146, 154, 155

— F —

Farm Services Administration, 6
Fast Mail and Express, the (passenger-mail train), 208
Finenger, Andreus, 33
First Street Yard, AT&SF RR, 246-247, 249
Flagstaff, Arizona, 208, 209°
Florida East Coast Line RR, 11
Fortieth Street Shops, C&NW RR, 92°, 93-95
Fortieth Street Yard, C&NW RR, 71, 72-73°
Ft. Madison, (Shopton), Iowa, 128, 134-136, 175
Ft. Sumner, New Mexico, 178

— G —

Galena Division, C&NW RR, 66, 79, 80
"Galloping Geese" (passenger railcars), 14°, 15
Gallup, New Mexico, 195, 202
Glorieta, Pass, 183, 211
Grants, New Mexico, 199

— H —

Halethorp, Maryland, 26
Hammond, Indiana, 75, 99, 100, 102, 103, 108, 109, 110, 111°, 112
Harper, Kansas, 159
Harvey House food service, 191, 248°, 249
Hiawatha, the (passenger train), 116
Hollem, Jack, 26
Holliday, Kansas, 143

— I —

Iden, New Mexico, 180
Illinois Central RR, 112, 118-121
Illinois Division, AT&SF RR, 123, 195
Illinois River, 123, 130
Indiana Harbor Belt RR, 5, 47, 75, 97-113
Interstate Commerce Commission, 135
Isleta, New Mexico, 189

— J —

Japanese trackworkers, 225

— K —

Kansas City, Missouri, 123, 143, 145, 146, 148, 152, 184
Kaw (Kansas) River, 143
Kingman, Arizona, 205, 208, 213
Kiowa, Kansas, 161-163
Kuhler, Otto, 139

— L —

Lange, Dorothea, 20
Lee, Russell, 11, 13, 18, 21
Los Angeles, California, 6, 152, 220, 235, 241, 246-249
Los Angeles Union Station, 216, 248°, 249
Los Pinos Mountains, the, 169
Ludlow, California, 217
Lynchburg, Virginia, 29

— M —

"Madam Queen" (AT&SF 2-10-4 No. 5000), 176, 177°, 179
Marceline, Missouri, 138
Melrose, New Mexico, 169
Michigan Central RR, (New York Central subsidiary), 99-100
Middle Division, AT&SF RR, 157
Missouri Division, AT&SF RR, 123
Missouri River, 123, 139-141
Montrose, Colorado, 17
Mountainair, New Mexico, 169
Mountaineer, the, (passenger train), 16°, 17
Mount San Antonio ("Old Baldy"), 226, 228°, 232°, 233

— N —

Nashville, Chattanooga, & St. Louis Railroad, 23
National Museum of Transport, St. Louis, Missouri, 39
Navajo Trackworkers, 205, 224°, 225
Needles, California, 205, 211, 214, 215
Nelson, Illinois, 91
New York Central RR, 75, 97, 99, 100
Norfolk & Western RR, 29, 79
Norpaul Yard, IHB RR, 103, 112
Northwestern Station, Chicago, 45, 71

— O —

Office of Defense Transportation, 35
Office of War Information, 5-6
Ouray, Colorado, 15

— P —

Pampa, Texas, 168, 173
Pecos River, the, 178
Pennsylvania RR, 32, 35, 41, 43, 112, 115, 143
Pitcairn Yard, P.R.R., 32
Plains Division, AT&SF RR, 173
Portsmouth, Branch, B&O RR, 22
Proviso Roundhouse, C&NW RR, 62-67
Proviso Yard, C&NW RR, 45-77, 78, 86

— R —

Raton Pass, 131, 169, 183, 187, 215

Richwood, West Virginia, 21
Rio Grande Division, AT&SF RR, 189
Rio Grande River Valley, 169
Rio Grande Southern Railroad, 13-15
Riordan, Arizona, 211, 212
Rothstein, Arthur, 17

— S —

San Bernardino, California, 197, 215, 216, 218, 221, 232-245, 247, 249
San Bernardino Mountains, 225
San Bernardino Roundhouse, AT&SF RR, 240°, 241, 242-243°, 244
San Bernardino Shops, AT&SF RR, 216, 236, 237°, 238, 239°
San Bernardino Yards, AT&SF RR, 228, 229-236, 247
San Diegan, the (passenger train), 25
San Diego, California, 25, 215, 220
San Francisco, Calif., 32, 220
San Juan, the (passenger train), 15
Scout, the, (passenger train), 208
Seligman, Arizona, 212
Shopton (Ft. Madison) Roundhouse, AT&SF RR, 134-136, 137°
Sibley, Missouri, 139
South Chicago Yard, I.C. RR, 118-121
Southern California Rwy. (subsidiary of the AT&SF RR), 215
Southern Pacific RR, 32, 45, 155, 215, 221
Southern Rwy., 25
St. Louis, Missouri, 17
St. Louis & San Francisco RR, (Frisco), 29-31, 143
Summit, California, 226, 227-228°
Super Chief, the (passenger train), 139, 191

— T —

Telluride, Colorado, 13
Terminal District, C&NW RR, 66
Texico, New Mexico, 175
Thoreau, New Mexico, 200
Topeka, Kansas, 143, 145, 148-152, 155, 212
Topeka Shops, AT&SF RR, 143, 148-152
Tulsa, Oklahoma, 29-31
Twin Cities 400, the, (passenger train), 71, 72-73°

— U —

Union Pacific RR, 45, 78, 123, 143, 215, 221, 229, 230, 236, 241
United States Railway Administration, 23
United States Sugar Co., 11
Utah Copper Company, 33, 34°

— V —

Vaughan, New Mexico, 183-187
Victorville, California, 221, 225
Virginia & Truckee RR, 12

— W —

War Production Board, the, 6, 118, 148, 195, 196
Waynoka, Oklahoma, 159, 164-166
Wellington, Kansas, 155-157, 169
Williams, Arizona, 210°, 211
Winslow, Arizona, 194°, 195, 204°, 205-208, 211, 212
Winslow Roundhouse, AT&SF RR, 207-208
Wisconsin Division, C&NW RR, 66

— Y —

Yeso, New Mexico, 179

— Z —

Zephyr, the (passenger train), 35, 37, 39, 78